D1250879

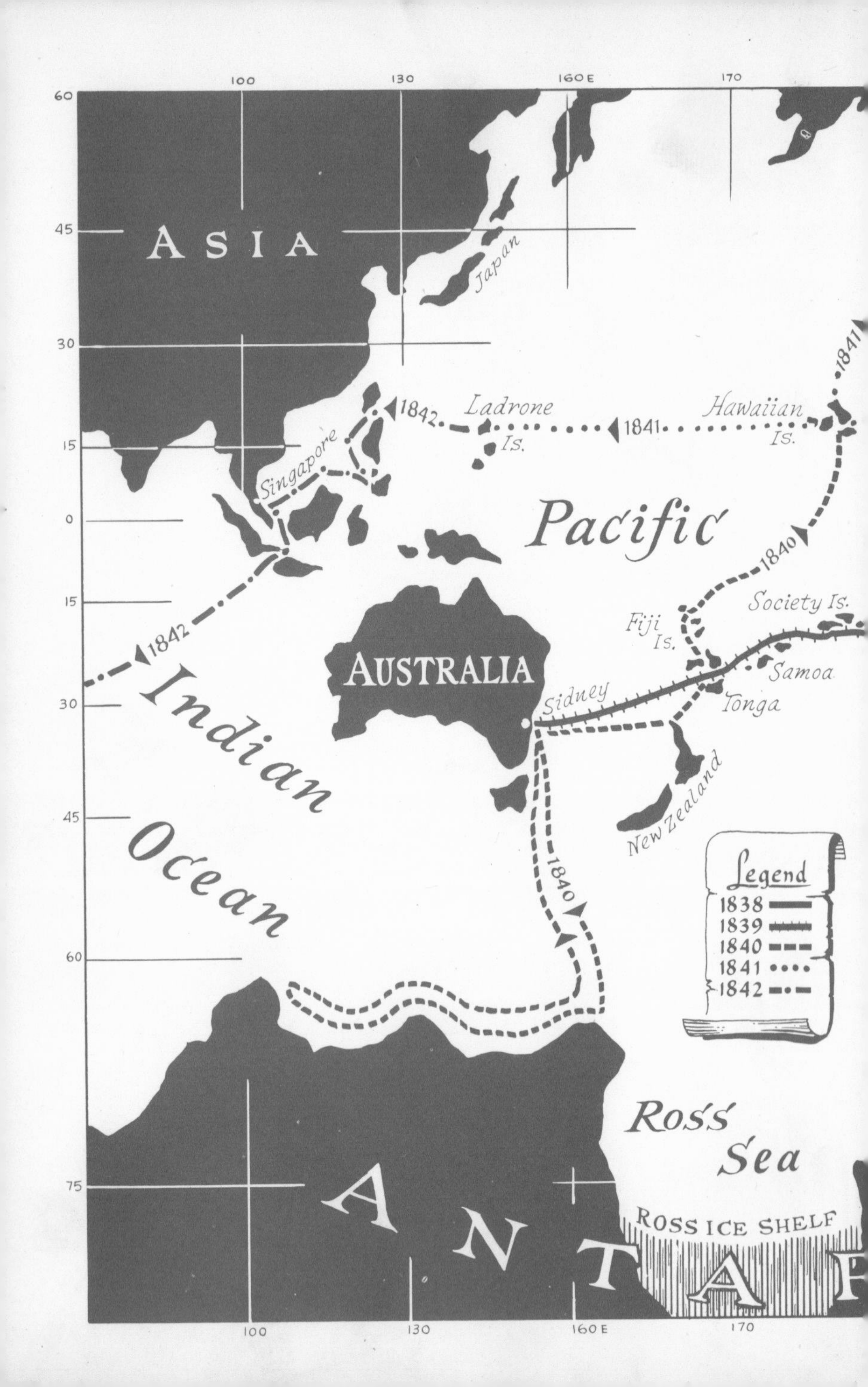

100
130
160 E
170
60
45
30
15
0
15
30
45
60
75
ASIA
Japan
Ladrone Is.
Hawaiian Is.
1842
1841
Singapore
Pacific
1840
Society Is.
Fiji Is.
AUSTRALIA
Samoa
Tonga
Sidney
New Zealand
Indian Ocean
Legend
1838
1839
1840
1841
1842
Ross Sea
ROSS ICE SHELF
ANTA

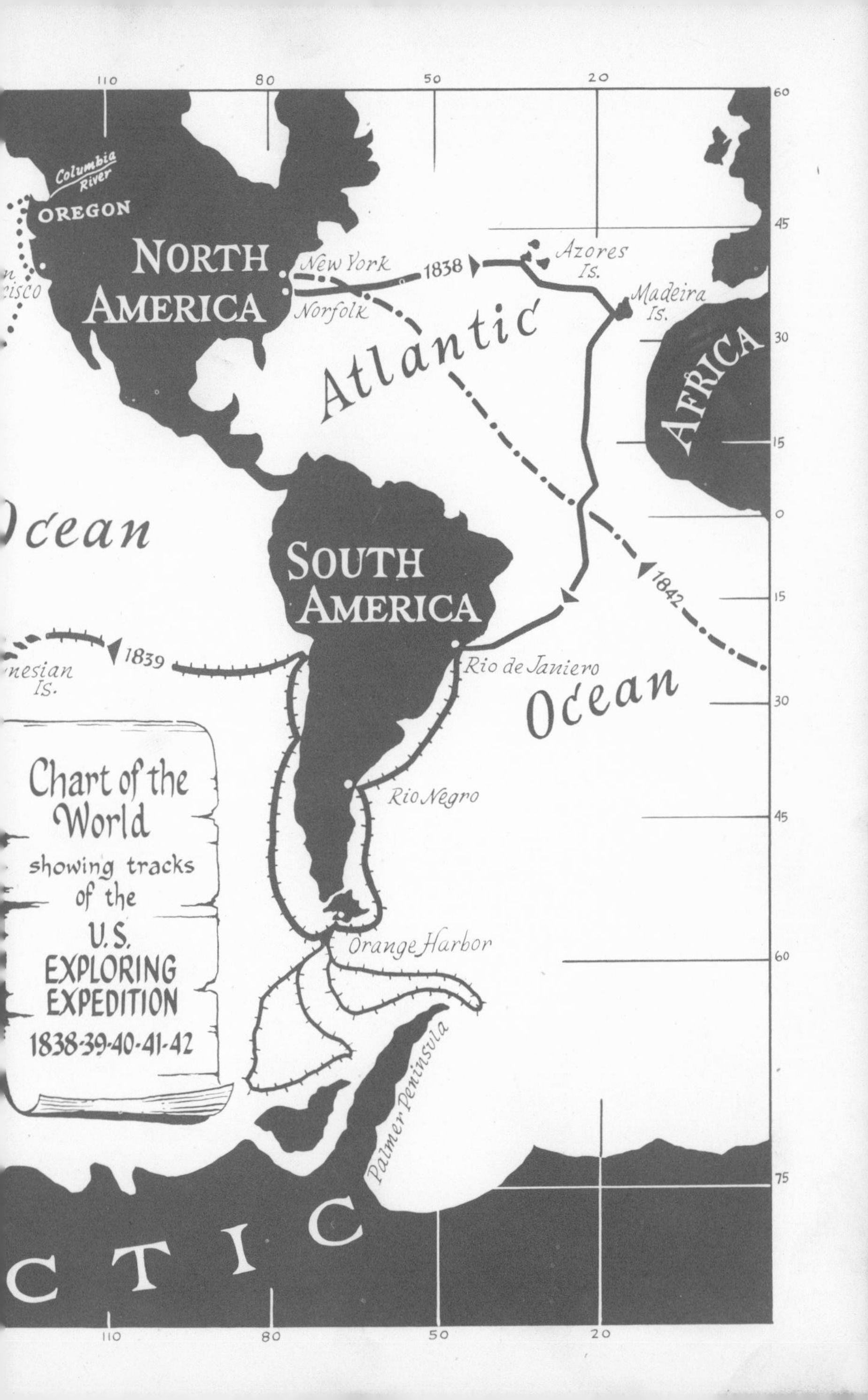
110
80
50
20
60
45
30
15
0
15
30
45
60
75
Columbia River
OREGON
NORTH AMERICA
New York
Norfolk
1838
Azores Is.
Madeira Is.
Atlantic
AFRICA
Ocean
SOUTH AMERICA
1842
1839
Rio de Janiero
Ocean
Rio Negro
Orange Harbor
Palmer Peninsula
Chart of the World showing tracks of the U.S. EXPLORING EXPEDITION 1838-39-40-41-42
CTIC
110
80
50
20

THE FORGOTTEN VOYAGE
of
CHARLES WILKES

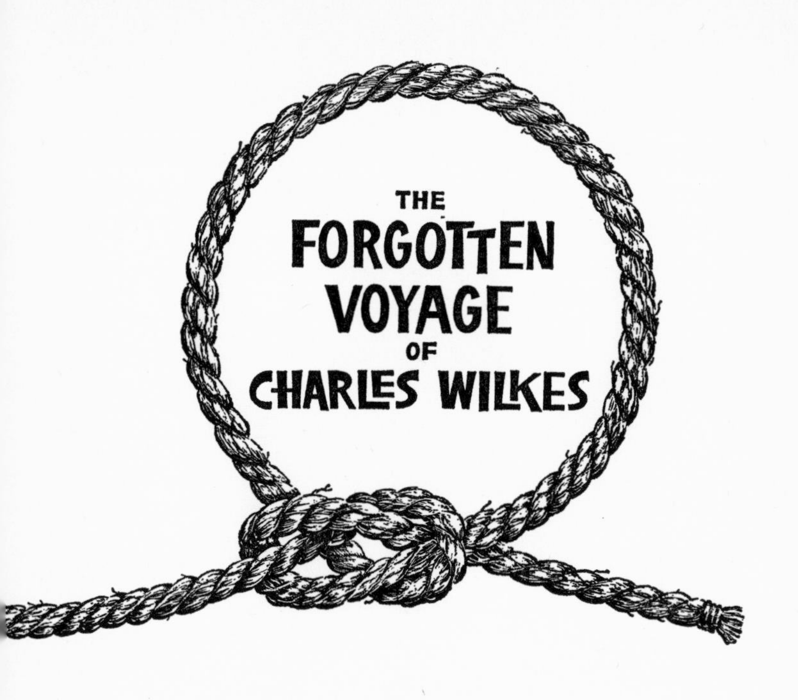

BY
WILLIAM BIXBY

Illustrations by JOHN FLYNN

DAVID McKAY COMPANY, INC.
NEW YORK

THE FORGOTTEN VOYAGE OF CHARLES WILKES

LIBRARY OF CONGRESS CATALOG CARD NUMBER: 66–12126

MANUFACTURED IN THE UNITED STATES OF AMERICA

PREFACE

EARLY in the nineteenth century, a great exploratory expedition was conceived by the United States Government. One of the chief arguments for it was to make sea lanes safe by charting unknown shoals and reefs in the areas of the South Atlantic, Antarctic and Pacific oceans. For by that time American commerce had begun to probe those waters in search of profit. Seal and whale hunters roamed the oceans. Many ships were wrecked on uncharted rocks and many contrary reports came back placing islands in various places on the charts. The extension and safeguarding of commerce formed an acceptable foundation for the venture which became known as the United States Exploring Expedition.

But President John Quincy Adams, in the last years of his office (1826–1828), dreamed also of a great scientific expedition—one which would place his young country in the forefront of scientific investigation in all areas of inquiry. Hitherto, England, France and Russia had led the way in geographical exploration of the Antarctic. The great voyages of Cook, Bellingshausen, Weddell, LePerouse and others had brought fame to the men and to their countries. Adams longed for an American opportunity to compete in geographical exploration.

He also wanted American scholars to search every

corner of the area called science during the voyage. Botany, zoology, anthropology, physics, astronomy, chemistry all offered challenges to the explorer-investigator. And so he planned for a corps of civilian scientists to accompany the expedition.

Adams could not persuade Congress to appropriate the money, however, and he left office with little hope that his dream would become reality. Andrew Jackson, his successor, took up the cause when he came to power but the project languished and Jackson himself left office before the expedition sailed.

Martin Van Buren was President when the expedition finally set sail in 1838. Congressional appropriation, however, did not permit the original grandiose scheme to be realized fully. Over the years, the question of who would lead the expedition had been decided and changed a number of times. Navy officers accepted the command and, when it became evident that Congress would delay again, went on to other duties.

When at last money was voted, the problem of selecting a Navy officer again arose. Over the heads of many higher ranking officers, Lieutenant Charles Wilkes was chosen. This instantly created service jealousies and—eventually—spelled trouble for Wilkes.

Wilkes was typical of the Navy officer of his day. He was from a family of wealth and social importance. He was trained to be a harsh disciplinarian who placed duty and station above all else. That he was, on more than one occasion, tactless and less than wise in the ways of handling people, was a product both of his nature and training.

But he prepared the expedition for sailing. It sailed and accomplished its mission. When Wilkes returned he was court-martialed and his subsequent career was as stormy as his voyage.

Then , curiously, Wilkes, his voyage, and the great wealth of scientific material his men had collected plus the geographical discoveries Wilkes made vanished from the national consciousness. This was due in part to the criticism leveled at him by explorers of other nations—principally the Englishman James Ross who was Wilkes' competitor during the actual years of his voyage. Wilkes' data were called false; his discoveries were discredited.

Yet today Antarcticians realize that Wilkes did indeed establish the fact that the Antarctic is a continent—not a series of islands surrounded by ice. Gradually, as misplaced national pride has been superseded by international cooperation in matters scientific, Wilkes has begun to emerge from obscurity and take his place in the front rank of United States explorers.

DEPARTURE

FROM the shore, the ships' departure was a grand sight. A visitor, mixing with the crowd there, would have been thrilled by the six ships that formed the squadron. Sails set, colors streaming from the main trucks, they moved in line with impeccable naval precision down Hampton Roads, Virginia, toward the open sea. Rails and rigging were lined with men—all waving farewell to the wives, children and friends along the shore. Women in the crowds waved handkerchiefs; men raised their hats as the flagship in the lead came abreast of them. Scores of children watched and waved, too. The sailors saw the gestures of good-bye but the distance was too great to see the women's tears.

The date was August 18, 1838. The departing ships formed the United States Naval Exploring Expedition outward bound on a voyage of four years. A casual observer might have congratulated everyone concerned on a good start. But if he had, he could not have been more mistaken. Government and Navy officials in Washington heaved great sighs of relief when they learned that the expedition had sailed—at last. Many Navy officers left behind nursed grudges—and they secretly swore to keep those grudges alive until the expedition returned, if it returned at all.

The commander of the expedition, Lieutenant Charles Wilkes, paced the quarterdeck of his flagship as it proceeded down Hampton Roads. He knew that in one sense he had left trouble behind, for there is nothing so final or conclusive as an outward-bound ship and a disappearing shore astern. But in another sense, he was taking a great deal of potential trouble with him. Aboard the ships were 440 officers and men, including a group of scientists and artists. These officers and men would be sailing for four years together. In moments of danger they would have to act in concert to avoid death. During long days of idleness against contrary winds or no winds at all, they would have to learn to stomach their boredom, execute their chores and remain cheerful. To do all this without trouble clearly was impossible.

More than this worried Wilkes, however. From a distance his ships looked formidable, trim and capable. But only from a distance. Work on refurnishing several of them had not been first-class. No extra strengthening of hulls had been carried out to prepare the ships for Antarctic ice—and the Antarctic was a most important area they were charged to explore. Although he did not know it on that bright August day, Wilkes was to discover that cold-weather clothing stored below was insufficient and second-rate.

His civilian scientists posed a problem, too. They were, to a man, landlubbers. Socially they presumed an equality with his officers—as they rightly should. But he knew his officers, who were, to a man, seasoned naval career officers, had only contempt for landlubbers. Who were these civilians with their butterfly nets, fish drags, spectacles, long-winded academic jargon, and books?

Lieutenant Wilkes had another quite personal worry. He had been promised, as expedition commander, the temporary rank of captain—as was his second in command, Lieutenant Hudson. Both men had, on the strength of that promise, ordered and purchased uniforms with the captain's stripes on the sleeves plus suitable braid and headgear. They were to be their country's representatives abroad for four long years. They would meet ambassadors in many ports, heads of state, captains, commodores and even admirals of other nations' navies. It could not be suitably done as a mere lieutenant. But the promise of elevation had not been kept. The Government, the Navy—someone—had disapproved the order. Perhaps even the President, Van Buren. It might not, Wilkes reflected, have been such a good idea to have said what he did when the President visited the squadron before its departure. He had mentioned that in getting the expedition under way, he was probably taking a white elephant off the Government's hands.

That he was, there was no doubt. But to have said it might not have been wise. Nonetheless it was done.

Wilkes knew he would have his hands more than full and that he had no one to turn to, no one "topside" who could give him advice. He had to act. In the matter of his captain's commission he acted promptly: He—and Hudson—would assume the rank of captain and wear the uniforms.

The instructions Wilkes was charged to execute were detailed and lengthy. Never before had the United States sent out an expedition of such size and scope.

Wilkes was to:

> Proceed to Rio de Janeiro and replenish supplies and search for "doubtful shoals" while en route.
>
> Examine the Rio Negro at about 41°S to determine "its resources and facilities for trade."
>
> Go to Tierra del Fuego on the southern tip of South America where he would select a harbor from which to launch his first attack on the Antarctic.
>
> Proceed to the Antarctic following the track of the famous English explorer James Weddell as "closely as possible" and reach as high a southern latitude as he could.
>
> Reform the squadron on the west coast of South

America and proceed into the Pacific checking shoals and islands marked "doubtful" on existing charts to the islands known as the Navigator Group.

Chart harbors and shoals of the Navigator Group and then proceed to the Society Islands and do the same thing—if time permitted.

Go to the Feejee Islands which he was "to examine with particular attention, with the view to the selection of a safe harbor, easy of access, and in every respect adapted to the reception of vessels of the United States engaged in the whale-fishery and the general commerce of these seas."

Arrange for supplies of fruits, vegetables and fresh provisions to be made available to vessels of the United States that would stop there in the future, "teaching the natives the modes of cultivation and encouraging them to raise hogs in great abundance."

Proceed to Sydney, Australia, and from there go south once more into the Antarctic "as far west as 45°E or to Enderby's Land, making your rendezvous on your return at Kerguelen's Land or the Isle of Desolation."

Sail for the Sandwich Islands where he would be met by a supply ship.

Go to the northwest coast of America making charts "first of the territory of the United States on the seaboard, and the Columbia River, and afterwards along the coast of California, with special reference to the Bay of San Francisco."

Sail to the coast of Japan taking in "as many doubtful islands as possible."

Enter the sea of Sooloo or Mindoro and determine whether or not there was a safe route through it which would "shorten the passage of our vessels to and from China."

Go to the Straits of Sunda and pass through the Straits of Billiton en route to Singapore—where another supply ship would meet his squadron.

Return to the United States by way of Cape of Good Hope "taking such a course as may be most likely to further the great purposes of the expedition."

During this entire journey, Wilkes was cautioned to make as good an impression for the United States upon the natives of civilized and savage countries as he could. He and his men were not to engage in trade—save for trinkets—with the natives nor were they to disturb the traditional customs of any tribe or society with whom they came in contact.

He was, in short, leading a scientific, exploratory and diplomatic expedition, grandly conceived, not well prepared, but, nevertheless, launched that day in August, 1838.

There is little wonder that Wilkes had premonitions of trouble ahead. He kept them to himself, as was proper, but in his private journal he confessed his feeling—it was, he wrote, "like one doomed to destruction."

THE SHIPS

Six vessels sailed from Hampton Roads that day. Of them, one was to be sent back before the expedition was over and two were to be wrecked and sunk in the far Pacific.

Wilkes' flagship was the sloop of war *Vincennes,* of 780 tons. She had only a single deck so Wilkes ordered another one built for the protection of the men and to give everyone more room.

The *Peacock* was another sloop of war, 650 tons, which should have been in good condition since she had made only two cruises prior to sailing with the expedition. But she was the least able ship that sailed.

The *Porpoise,* a brig of 230 tons, had been used by Wilkes before and he had had it altered by building a poop-cabin and forecastle on her deck.

With these three large vessels were two small, light ships and a supply vessel. The *Sea Gull* and *Flying Fish* were taken as shallow draft vessels to move in shoal water while exploring and charting the islands of the Pacific and the coasts of California and Oregon. The only thing that worried Wilkes about them at the outset was whether or not they could round Cape Horn successfully. They were 110 and 96 tons respectively.

The supply ship, *Relief,* was a sound vessel that had been designed as a store ship by the Navy. But the *Relief* had one drawback that forced Wilkes to change plans several times—she was so slow she hampered the progress of the other ships.

THE MEN

To man the ships and accomplish the purposes of the expedition, 440 officers and men had been chosen. Navy personnel, 418 officers and men up to and including Wilkes himself, were all accustomed to the rigors of the service. Enlisted men knew that should discipline come, it would arrive as a set of whistling knotted thongs tied to a short wooden handle: the cat-o'-nine-tails applied to their bared backs. The number of lashes would be set by the degree of infraction of the rules. For major crimes, keel-hauling still was a punishment they had to face: being hauled by a line beneath the ship from port to starboard or stem to stern. It was a punishment few survived and those who did frequently died from infected lacerations caused by barnacles on the ship's bottom.

Non-commissioned officers fared better. Their value to the precise and efficient running of a ship was understood by everyone from Wilkes on down. All these men were veterans of the service and their experience and skill in handling crews, in keeping discipline and a "tight ship" could save many situations. Without their cooperation, Wilkes knew he would have more trouble than otherwise.

Commissioned officers—career naval officers of that time—were taken from the top ranks of society as was Wilkes. Many were members of fading aristocratic families and pride, position, rank and protocol concerned them constantly.

The remainder of the men aboard the six ships were the scientists to whom little mattered but their specialty: anthropology, ornithology, geography, zoology or oceanography. They cheerfully admitted they knew little of the seafaring life. Yet among them were names destined to become famous: James Dwight Dana, Asa Gray, Charles Pickering, Titian R. Peale. Many of the men were capable not only in their specialty but also in the business of sketching and painting of specimens, for the day of the camera had not arrived and nearly everyone interested in biological, cartographic or botanical study had taken pains to become proficient enough to record by drawing what was seen. There were also two expedition artists—Alfred T. Agate and Joseph Drayton, plus a philologist to study the languages of primitive peoples encountered, Horatio Hale.

Death would strike among officers and men alike in the four years that lay ahead. Sickness would cause the discharge of several and discipline would account for the detachment of others (and these men would make their way homeward, returning to bring their version of the complaint that caused their discharge, storing more trouble for Wilkes in the years after his return).

PORPOISE IN A GALE

THE Virginia coast still lay in sight astern when Wilkes ordered the chaplain to hold the first service for officers and men. When it was over everyone turned their attention to the first of the problems facing them: reaching the first landfall.

Wilkes planned to take all ships to the Island of Madeira off the west coast of Africa and then southwest to Rio de Janeiro. This zigzag course was customary in those days of sail but the plan had to be altered almost at once.

The supply ship *Relief,* rolling slowly in the Atlantic swells, could not keep pace with the rest of the squadron and Wilkes signaled for her to proceed on her own to the Cape Verde Islands where she could water ship and then set sail for Rio. The speed of this lumbering ship was so low she required nearly three times as long to travel from the United States to Rio than faster vessels of her day.

Squadrons of that time, traveling on extended cruises,

frequently faced the problem of keeping together. Signal flags were the principal means of communication between them and, before such a squadron sailed, certain rendezvous points were agreed upon. For in gales or during night hours, ships could separate and when the storm subsided or dawn came on the sea, a captain could scan the horizon vainly for sight of his companions. This happened—the first of many times—on the squadron's first leg of the journey. A squall separated the squadron and Wilkes lost sight of the *Flying Fish* and the *Peacock* during the night of storm. He proceeded, however, since both captains of the missing ships had orders to make Madeira the first landfall.

Aboard the *Vincennes,* Wilkes was discovering the extent of the problems facing him. And a few days after the ships put to sea, an incident occurred that would have dismayed a more superstitious man than the Commander.

A maintopman was loosing the topgallant sail when he was caught by the buntline and dragged over the yard. Men on deck saw him swinging back and forth by his neck, motionless. Two men raced aloft and tried to rescue their shipmate. But they, too, appeared to be in danger of being dragged into the same position. Several other hands sprang to their help. The man who had been hanging by his neck finally was lowered to the deck and, to everyone's relief, found to be alive.

Wilkes had had no time to brood on the incident for his hands were already full. One of the chief sources of trouble came from the fact that Wilkes was junior in rank to many of the officers serving under him. His service time did not equal theirs and so, among his officers, he detected a certain coolness. Hudson, his second in command, was an officer of longer service than Wilkes, and he had been persuaded to sign on as second only after much persuasion by Navy authorities.

But on that first day out of Hampton Roads, Wilkes showed everyone he meant to run the expedition without regard to the unusual situation of a junior officer ordering seniors about. One officer, actually junior to Wilkes, was muffing the job of assigning men and non-commissioned officers to their various duties. Wilkes jumped in, ordered the bungling officer aside and did the job quickly and expertly.

The men approved, but in the wardroom a number of officers muttered among themselves.

This incident gave Wilkes concern about the seaworthiness of his officers and at Madeira he had grave fears about the seaworthiness of the *Peacock*. On inspection, her commander found that much repair work had been overlooked. He already had had to replace the fore and cross-jack-yards after the ship had been repaired by shipyard workers. At Madeira, Captain Hudson of the *Peacock* discovered much of the iron work in the bilge was rusted beyond use. He presented Wilkes with an iron hoop from one of the pumps which was nothing more than a ring of rust. Wilkes sent this example and a letter to the Secretary of the Navy—an act described as "impudent" and one that was not forgotten in Washington.

On reaching Rio de Janeiro, more ship trouble came to light, and further delay for the squadron. Several of the vessels had to undergo repairs and once again the *Peacock* led them all in unseaworthiness. The head of the mizzenmast had to be amputated, eighteen inches of it, because of a flaw which turned out to be a large cavity produced by rot. Shipyard workers in the United States had merely stuffed the hole with rope ends and putty, painted it over and declared the mizzenmast fit.

Other ships of the squadron also needed repairs before venturing into higher southern latitudes and Wilkes fretted in Rio while the work was done. But it was not until early in January, 1839, that all ships were ready to sail—yet even with that repair work, Wilkes anticipated more breakdowns.

He had no sooner put his ships in order and prepared to sail than trouble with his men began again. A slave ship under English colors, *The Fox,* had put into the harbor at Rio and two of Wilkes' men were missing. Rumor along the waterfront had it that they had signed on the slaver, deserting the squadron. Wilkes ordered the *Porpoise* to drop down to the mouth of the harbor where the slaver was anchored and investigate. And although the captain of *The Fox* denied taking on any new hands, a search disclosed the missing seamen who were brought back to their ships.

On January 6, Wilkes' ships finally got underway and stood out to sea. In dropping down the harbor toward the next leg of their voyage, they passed the *U. S. S.*

Independence then visiting Rio and the captain of that warship ordered his men to yards and rail where they cheered the departing squadron. And then, with land once more behind him, Wilkes had only to face the sea.

The government's instructions called for Wilkes to survey the mouth of the Rio Negro or Black River. Sailing down the coast of South America toward that destination, the squadron met the first ominous sign of the Antarctic. The ships were proceeding southward off the mouth of Rio de la Plata on the evening of January 19. All were in sight of one another as the sun set and watch officers had just time to notice that the sea was discolored before the nightfall. The sea became glowingly phosphorescent in the darkness and the wake of each ship streamed astern like a trail of fire. Lightning flickered in a looming bank of clouds far to the west. At ten o'clock the ships found themselves in an inexplicable fog. It arrived suddenly. One moment the squadron sailed in clear seas with good visibility. The next, a lookout could scarcely see his own ship's bowsprit. At the moment the fog appeared, the temperature of both the air and water dropped a full ten degrees. The cold clammy wisps of haze made watch officers shiver. The wind died to a light breeze and the sea was smooth as glass. Orders to shorten sail rang out and the decks drummed to the sound of hurrying feet. Wilkes ordered soundings taken to discover if the squadron were running into shoal water, some uncharted reef or island. But a hundred fifty fathoms of line dropped overside failed to find bottom. All sail was set to take advantage of the light airs. By this time the ships were sailing in close order, moving through the cold, phosphorescent sea.

The fog thickened the next day and the ships proceeded cautiously, still in the cold air. Until January 23 the odd temperature persisted and when at last it rose to a more normal height, Wilkes was convinced that they had all felt the breath of the Antarctic. For although they were in relatively low latitude (38°55′S), records showed that gigantic icebergs from the south had been sighted that far north before. This, and only this, Wilkes reasoned, could have accounted for the sudden drop in temperature, the inexplicable fog and the sudden lapse of the wind. For only icebergs could lower the water temperature, only sailing in the lee of those towering cliffs of ice could cut off a wind, only a condensation of water vapor in the colder air could produce the unusual fog.

When the survey of the Rio Negro estuary had been completed, the squadron set sail southward again. Its destination was Orange Harbor on the southern tip of South America on the western side of dread Cape Horn. As the ships moved daily into higher southern latitudes, more and more indications came to commanders of the trials the Antarctic had in store for them. The two smaller ships, *Flying Fish* and *Sea Gull,* found difficulty in staying with the larger *Vincennes, Peacock* and *Porpoise.* They had to shorten sail and proceed at a slower pace which put them at a disadvantage in the increasingly boisterous weather. Under shortened sail, they lurched, pitched and rolled, rising and falling on the waves. Wilkes soon realized he was risking more damage to those smaller vessels and he ordered them to proceed at their own pace to Orange Harbor where all vessels would rendezvous.

On February 13, the three large ships of the squadron sighted Staten Island and Cape St. Diego at the tip of the continent. With favoring tide, the *Vincennes, Peacock* and *Porpoise* sailed through the Straits of Le Maire in three hours, the men and officers alike marveling at the wild, high lands, desolate and driven by winds and the sea—silent outposts of the continent to the north.

On taking a sounding east of Cape Horn, Wilkes found the water temperature at the surface to be 44°F but at a depth of 450 fathoms (2700 feet) it was 28°F. Antarctic currents far beneath the ships brought the cold water that far north.

New sky phenomena captured their attention. On February 16 a young lieutenant aboard the *Porpoise* observed and sketched a remarkable example of parhelion. With the sun but eight degrees above the horizon, he saw three images of it. The true sun was the faintest image. Below it about one diameter, a brilliant mock sun glowed and on the same level but far to the right, another mock sun, fainter but sparkling with the colors of the spectrum and brushed with a halo of light also glowed across the southern seas. Refraction of light through layers of air of varying density causes such images and their unreality lingers long in the minds of men who see them for the first time.

The same is true of mirages. Just west of Cape Horn

(which Wilkes sailed within two miles of and found the weather delightful) officers of the *Vincennes* gazing toward the *Peacock* sailing a few miles away observed not one but three ships. The first was the hull of the *Peacock* safely settled in the ocean—but her masts and sails were displaced upward a little by mirage and a band of light separated her hull from her superstructure. Above this were two more clear images of the ship—one high in the air and right side up, another below that and upside down.

Wilkes sent a man aloft to take the masthead temperature at the same time he measured the temperature at deck level. Comparison of the readings showed deck temperature to be 54° while at the masthead it was 62°. A warmer layer of air was aloft while colder air hovered above the sea's surface and light refracted through these various layers of warm and cold air produced the ship's images "miraged up" above the horizon.

Such images and displacements are common in Antarctic latitudes and as the months and years were to pass, Wilkes would find himself being made the victim of such phenomena in quite unexpected ways.

All ships made Orange Harbor safely. Even the slow *Relief* was there having been dispatched from Rio de Janeiro long before. The harbor itself was little more than a shelter among the off-shore islands west of Nassau Bay and not far from Cape Horn itself. But in the lee of these islands, almost surrounded by high cliffs, the ships were comparatively safe for the first major move of the expedition: a thrust into the Antarctic before winter froze the surface of all the far southern seas.

Wilkes arrived in Orange Harbor in February. For ships in those latitudes, this is extremely late in the season. Wilkes himself had fretted at the delays, precisely because of this time element. His orders called for exploration in the quadrant of the Antarctic directly below South America and those waters are navigable only during the Antarctic summer—roughly November to April. Frustrating delays reaching all the way back to the navy yards in Virginia had begun to threaten the success of the exploring expedition and very little had happened since the departure from Hampton Roads to improve the situation.

Accordingly, Wilkes wasted no time in Orange Harbor.

His plan called for separation of the squadron since there was little point in taking all ships in one direction to the same place for exploration. So Wilkes divided his ships in this manner:

The *Porpoise* (with Wilkes aboard) and the tender *Sea Gull* were to sail south and east to Palmer Peninsula (then called Palmer's Land) and explore as far south as possible along the eastern coast of that large, island-surrounded extension of the continent.

The *Peacock,* under Captain Hudson, with the tender *Flying Fish* were to sail south and west into what is now called Bellingshausen Sea and attempt to beat the *ne plus ultra* or farthest south of the great eighteenth-century English explorer, James Cook.

The *Relief* was to proceed eastward into the Straits of Magellan with many of the scientific corps aboard to gather data from that little-known area.

Wilkes' flagship, the *Vincennes,* was to remain in Orange Harbor and the scientists remaining aboard her were to examine the country and people surrounding that anchorage.

First Southern Voyage of the Porpoise: At 7 A.M. on February 25, the *Porpoise* stood out of the harbor with the *Sea Gull* following. Men aboard the other ships gave their departing fellows a cheer but Wilkes felt the ominous breath of the Antarctic close on him. He was depressed, for he knew that in ordering the ships to sail as he had done, he was inviting both danger and disaster. The southern ocean and the ice fields of the Antarctic shores and seas are treacherous.

On the first day out of the harbor, light breezes and mild weather were pleasant but unproductive. Late that afternoon, however, a bank of cumulus clouds spread rapidly over the southwestern horizon and a blinding squall struck the two ships. Sails filled and the sea foamed under the bowsprits driving the vessels south.

The ships were heading across Drake Passage, that relatively narrow corridor of sea separating the tip of South America and the northernmost reaches of Antarctica. It is the oceanic division of the Pacific and Atlantic Oceans and for 360°—completely around the world in that latitude—no land mass interrupts the flowing sea or the rushing wind. It is the stormiest portion of all the world's oceans and great wave patterns built by winds thousands of miles away build to even greater heights as new winds arise and the pattern of waves sweeps on.

Wilkes, aboard the *Porpoise,* measured the speed and height of the waves he encountered by sighting on the *Sea Gull* which was sailing behind the larger ship. Wilkes had the log heaved with a wooden chip attached which floated from the bow of the *Porpoise* alongside and then astern as the line was paid out more rapidly than the chip was moving. By timing the chip until it reached the crest of the first following wave, and noting the fact that a certain time was required for the waves to reach the *Sea Gull* he calculated the speed of the wave pattern (after accounting for the speed of his own ship through the water which was about eight knots). Then by sighting on the *Sea Gull* when she was down in the trough of a wave, Wilkes saw where the wave crest intersected his view of the *Sea Gull*'s mast. This gave him the wave height. The speed of wave progression was determined at 26½ miles per hour and the height of the waves at 32 feet. It was a relatively mild day in Drake Passage.

Water temperature dropped to 32° on March first. Snow flurries enveloped the ships and the men sighted their first icebergs. They were large, though worn by much sea action, and, as Wilkes noted, they were to see many larger ones later but these first sentinels of the southern regions still inspired awe in the newcomers.

As the ships proceeded, the birds of the Antarctic appeared: the albatross, that wanderer of the ocean, grey and black petrels and Cape pigeons. The birds circled the ships, staring curiously at the intruders.

Wilkes watched the increasing number of icebergs, the ice floes riding low in the water, and decided that, when darkness fell, his only recourse was to heave to and not try to sail during the night. For one collision with either a berg or a large floe would sink his ships. By March, penguins had made their appearance. They swam beside the ships, eying them and screaming among themselves at so strange a sight.

By eight o'clock on the morning of the third, the *Porpoise* and *Sea Gull* had moved around the tip of Palmer's Land and were sailing south along the eastern coast amid icebergs that became larger and more numerous with each passing mile. It was here that Wilkes and his men met for the first time the large, flat, tabular icebergs so characteristic of high southern latitudes. Wilkes reported that the sea was literally studded with them. Their towering sides rose 200 feet into the cold air and the sea dashed against them sending showers of spray high above the rigging of the ships. Some were white shimmering masses of ice while others were opal or emerald green. A few showed up on the horizon that were black.

As the ice became thicker, Wilkes was forced to order both ships to alter course to try to get clear of the bergs. They had ventured within sight of Mt. Hope on the eastern shores of Palmer Peninsula. At nightfall, the watch officer counted eight "ice islands," as they were termed by the men, in sight as the sun went down. Wilkes again ordered both vessels to heave to during darkness. Fog as well as darkness obscured the ice. As the temperature fell that night, the men were supplied with cold-weather clothing that, for the first time, was brought out of the holds.

The men found that the inferior materials did not protect them. Wilkes looked the clothing over and realized that, once again, he and his men had been cheated—not only cheated but placed in grave danger. The clothing was not as good as the samples Wilkes had been shown by contractors back in the United States. Wilkes did not know whether the contractors or the equipment inspectors were at fault—and it made little difference that night of cold and darkness as the two ships rode the sea with furled sails.

A storm rose from the southwest, sending spray high in the rigging, coating masts and spars with ice. Water on the decks quickly froze, covering them with a thick slab of ice. And out of the darkness came the icebergs. Orders sent the shivering men aloft to set sails; the helmsmen struggled with the ice-coated wheel trying to follow commands that would keep the ships from being crushed by ice.

That night of suffering passed, but when daylight came the storm increased. Fog swirled over the waves and the danger from driving ice continued. Wilkes watched his shivering men trying to handle sail, climbing the ice-coated rigging and making their way out on the yards, their feet sending down showers of ice from the footrope.

He knew there was no hope of going farther south so late in the season. Aboard the *Porpoise,* the men were in poor condition and already incipient scurvy had broken out among the crew. But whatever the situation was on the large vessel, Wilkes knew it was far worse on the small *Sea Gull.* He ordered the tender back to Orange Harbor and the *Porpoise* parted company with her.

Wilkes' ship drove north through fog and increasing snow. Lookouts strained for a sight of icebergs and, on many occasions, their cries coming down through the fog to the helmsmen narrowly averted disaster. By March 7, the ship was running through fog well to the north of Palmer Peninsula and when it lifted, black cliffs of rock loomed dead ahead. The wheel spun quickly and the ship changed course just in time to escape being splintered on the inhospitable shores of Elephant Island. A quick check of the navigator's log from the last-known position showed the ship had been driven nearly fifty miles eastward by strong, uncharted currents flowing past the tip of Palmer Peninsula in Drake Passage.

Sailing north again, through increasingly bitter winter weather, Wilkes reached the Straits of Le Maire on March 16. The ship was out of the grip of the Antarctic but had entered the stormy seas surrounding Cape Horn.

The *Porpoise* anchored in Good Success Bay and two boats took Wilkes and an exploring party ashore. They landed safely but during their stay the surf increased and a storm threatened. Wilkes in one boat got safely off but the second boat foundered in the surf, spilling the men into the icy water. They struggled ashore safely and stood lining the beach, waiting for help.

Back aboard his ship, Wilkes surveyed the situation. The surf had risen higher and there was no way to rescue the men. But, somehow, supplies of food had to reach them.

Two boats left the *Porpoise* under the command of Lieutenant Hartstein. Wilkes had ordered the young officer to lash provisions aboard one boat and try to heave or float a line ashore so the stranded men could haul the provision boat through the surf.

This proved impossible and Wilkes saw, to his dismay, four men including the lieutenant get aboard the provision boat and prepare to run the surf. Even as he watched, the boat broached and rolled over in the pounding waves. All four men vanished.

The men in the second boat began rowing frantically and Wilkes saw them pick up two survivors. Watching through his glass, he tried to count the number of men on shore. They seemed to have increased but he could not be certain. The surviving boat came alongside and Lieutenant Hartstein and one seaman, Samuel Stretch, were lifted aboard. Both were near total exhaustion and when they were strong enough to speak, Wilkes learned that the other two men had managed to swim ashore.

The surf now had grown to mountainous heights and the storm was driving the *Porpoise* dangerously near the rocky shoals. Wilkes ordered his ship out to sea until the storm passed and the surf subsided. There was little else he could do. Before leaving, the crew of the *Porpoise* tried every conceivable trick to put provisions ashore for their stranded comrades. They even tried to fly a kite with a line attached. That attempt failed and the *Porpoise* had to leave with Wilkes still worrying about his stranded shivering men.

Five days of cruising close-hauled, riding out the storm did little to relieve the commander's anxiety and on the sixth day after the accident, the *Porpoise* returned to Good Success Bay. The storm had died and the surf was only a pleasant murmur on the rocky beach. A boat put out from the ship. It landed easily bringing the men back to the ship. Only then did Wilkes learn that the original provision boat had somehow reached shore, rolling over and over in the waves, and that the men had had food on which to survive. Thankfully, Wilkes ordered the ship to return to Orange Bay.

First southern voyage of the Peacock: Three hours after the *Porpoise* left Orange Harbor for her first encounter with the Antarctic, Captain Hudson, aboard the *Peacock* and accompanied by the tender *Flying Fish,* stood out to sea. The gale, however, that had driven the *Porpoise* southward on her journey, delayed Hudson's ship for a day and not until the twenty-sixth of February did she begin her cruise into southern waters.

The least sound vessel in the entire squadron, the *Peacock,* began immediately to have her share of bad luck. By midafternoon of their first day at sea, they were under storm sails and almost immediately they lost sight of their tender, the *Flying Fish*. During the storm, the unseaworthiness of the *Peacock* became painfully evident. Timbers began to work; the ports below deck could not be closed tightly and with every roll of the laboring ship, water streamed into her hull soaking the men's quarters and all their gear. Pumps were manned. They managed to keep up with the inflow of water—but nothing could be done to stop that cascade of icy Antarctic ocean from threatening the ship constantly.

On March 9, a seaman, William Stewart, captain of the maintop, was out on a yard handling sail when he slipped and fell. For a moment those on deck expected to see him shattered on the wood beneath their feet, but a sudden lurch of the ship and a last touch of the footrope sent him into the stormy water. He struck head first and lost consciousness. All that kept him afloat were his large boots and these held him upside down in the water so that only they were visible. The height of the waves made it impossible to lower a boat and his shipmates watched helplessly from the deck. One sailor, in desperation, threw out a line and lassoed the man's feet. He was hauled back aboard the *Peacock* but in his fall and stay in the water he had ruptured his lungs. Two days later he died.

On March 17 and 18, the *Peacock*, still vainly searching for the lost tender *Flying Fish*, ran into a true Antarctic gale. Rigging, yards and spars and decks were soon covered in an impenetrable casing of ice. Still the water poured in through the ports. The men were all soaked through and there was no place where they could dry out or get dry clothing.

Deep in Bellingshausen Sea, the *Peacock* ran into icebergs, storms and fog. During the periods when fog blanketed the ship she could not sail for fear of striking a berg. Nor could she move at night. But Captain Hudson inched his way southward in the increasingly bad weather. At nights, when it was clear, the strange colorful aurora australis, counterpart of aurora borealis in the northern hemisphere, lighted the entire southern sky. On March 25, the weather cleared during daylight hours sufficiently to take a fix on the sun. The navigator placed the ship at 69° South Latitude, 97°58′ West Longitude. It was on this spot that the *Peacock* miraculously located the *Flying Fish*.

Lieutenant Walker, her commander, came aboard the *Peacock* and reported his adventures to Captain Hudson. On losing sight of the *Peacock*, the smaller vessel had sailed to all appointed positions for rendezvous but without success. Lieutenant Walker had then turned the bow of the small ship south. This smallest of the squadron ships was trying to reach farther south into Antarctic waters than anyone in history.

Unknown to Lieutenant Walker—or anyone else at that time—they were in precisely the wrong position to get very far south. For although they were in Bellingshausen Sea they were directly north of a headland reaching out into the sea called Thurston Peninsula. In some sectors of the Antarctic, ice fields attached to the shore stretch for miles into the ocean and prevent any ship's passage. This was the case with the *Flying Fish*. On March 17, Lieutenant Walker began his struggle south. They already were among giant icebergs and on the next day they sighted sea ice and old pieces of bergs that were discolored, as though they recently had been attached to land. A sounding was taken but no bottom found to a depth of 100 fathoms. The ship was blanketed by fog and when it lifted during that day, the officers and men of the tender stared southward in amazement. They faced a wall of ice fifteeen to twenty feet high extending east and west to the horizon and south as far as anyone could see from the masthead. The way south was blocked.

Lieutenant Walker turned north into open water and then altered course again for another probe southward along another meridian of longitude. The small ship sailed not only among icebergs, but also in the midst of herds of whales, whales so numerous that there was danger of the ship's colliding with those great mammals of the sea—some of which were larger than the ship itself. Lieutenant Walker ordered several of his ten-man crew to stand forward with boat hooks to try to fend off in case one of the leviathans blocked their way.

Still Walker pressed the ship southward. They passed the farthest south positions of the earlier French and Russian explorers and were hoping to beat Cook's record of 71°10′ South. By this time, crew and officers were wet and weary beyond imagining. Everything below deck was awash—books, furniture, bedding and clothes. A jib had been split by the gale winds, a binnacle had washed overboard, and two men lay injured in their bunks below without the service of a doctor.

By the twenty-fourth, the *Flying Fish* had sailed to 70°14′ South—less than one degree from Cook's record. Later that day a man at the masthead reported the "appearance of land" to southward. The small schooner was fighting among huge ice islands that towered far above the masts and with great thickening fields of ice. The lookout's view was suddenly blotted out as a snowstorm struck the vessel. The temperature began to drop and Walker feared the ice would imprison them in the pack that began to form around his ship. He ordered the *Flying Fish* about and set a northward course. It was too late in the season to try further. The jaws of the Antarctic were about to snap shut. Struggling continuously with the ice, the *Flying Fish* inched her way toward open water and when she appeared within range of the *Peacock* she was a battered, ice-coated blob on the dark Antarctic seas.

Aboard the *Peacock,* Captain Hudson, Lieutenant Walker and the other officers reviewed their position. It was incredibly late to be sailing in those waters. Approaching winter could freeze them in until the following spring and, as everyone knew, the *Peacock* was in poor shape and there were no provisions aboard the *Flying Fish* to get men through a winter in the Antarctic ice.

Captain Hudson came to the conclusion that his ships had done all they possibly could in those late months and he ordered both ships to head north, away from the ice.

On the first of April at 60°12′ S. Latitude; 84°20′ W. Longitude the *Peacock* parted company with the *Flying Fish*. Hudson ordered Lieutenant Walker to Orange Harbor while the *Peacock* proceeded directly to the next rendezvous point on the squadron's schedule—Valparaiso, Chile.

The voyage of the Relief: Although the supply ship of Wilkes' squadron was the slowest vessel he had, he knew it would serve for a short voyage into the little-known area of the Straits of Magellan. Not only could soundings be taken and currents and tides studied, but scientists could land to gather specimens of both plant and animal life, geologists could examine the structure of those far southern islands that make up the lower end of South America.

The *Relief* weighed anchor and left Orange Harbor on February 26, setting a southeasterly course to reach the Magellanic Straits and specifically to enter Brecknock Passage and Cockburn Sound. Almost instantly the famed Cape Horn weather struck the ship and kept her off the coast, tacking back and forth trying to make headway toward her destination. For 20 days the *Relief* could not overcome the contrary winds but on the seventeenth of March, Lieutenant Commandant Long, her captain, decided to run for an anchorage in the lee of Noir Island. The gale-force winds from the southwest still buffeted the ship and there was fog intermixed with sudden hail squalls which cut down visibility. As the ship careened through the heavy seas, Long spotted his goal of the moment, Noir Island, about 12 miles distant. What he did not see, however, were Tower Rocks, lying in his path. These rocks jutted from the stormy sea and the wave patterns broke completely over them. Running down to what he hoped would be a safe anchorage to ride out the storm, the lookout saw Tower Rocks looming before the ship. A shout and a quick turn of the helm averted disaster. The ship sailed close by the rocks and turned at last to safety in the lee of the island.

Yet it was less of a safe place than Long had hoped for. The great waves of Drake Passage swirled completely around the island and swept into the bay in which the *Relief* sought shelter.

So great was the sea that Long let go three anchors to hold the ship in 17 fathoms of water. Two days later the weather cleared enough for the men to see the snow-capped peak of Noir Island and, as the wind slacked off, they made ready to land and begin their mission. But before they could get boats lowered, the wind increased and Long had to let go a fourth anchor. Then a wind shift toward the southeast put the *Relief* in an exposed position and all on watch kept glancing worriedly astern where a large rock showed above the white surf. Should the anchors not hold or the chains break, everyone knew the *Relief* would be on that rock in a matter of seconds.

On the morning of March 20 with the storm still raging, the watch discovered one of the anchor chains had parted. They hove it in and let go still another anchor on a new chain. The wind hurled itself on shore, howling through the mouth of the small bay. During that night no one slept. Mingled with the sound of the wind was the ominous noise of anchor chains dragging on the rocky bottom. By midnight, the ship had moved closer to the rock, despite the anchors, but the current had also moved the ship to one side of it—and the *Relief* cleared that danger. A reef to leeward posed another threat, however, and everyone knew there would be no survivors if they struck it. During the darkness of that stormy night, one great wave crashed over the bow of the ship and all anchor chains parted. The ship drifted at the mercy of current and wind. Long and his men watched helplessly. The current was the main factor determining the ship's direction and it carried the vessel clear of the reef. The great swirl of water took the ship around a point of the island and as soon as she cleared all jutting rocks and headlands, Long ordered more sail set. By daybreak the ship was wallowing in heavy seas off Cape Gloucester. Hurrying westward from the Straits of Magellan, the ship headed for Valparaiso, Chile, where she arrived without anchors on April 13. Long signaled the news of his loss of anchors which meant he could not moor his ship safely in the harbor, and the commander of a British man-o'-war courteously sent over spares from his supply for the hapless *Relief*.

Lieutenant Commandant Long's orders had been to return to Orange Harbor rather than proceed to Valparaiso but he left the Magellanic Straits so late that he thought it advisable to proceed directly to the next major rendezvous point. And logical though his action was, it contributed indirectly to the first major disaster of the expedition.

Wilkes, once more aboard the *Vincennes* in Orange Harbor left that anchorage on April 20 in company with the *Porpoise*. He knew the *Peacock* had gone directly to Valparaiso and only the missing *Relief* was on his mind. He did not want to delay the expedition longer and so he left after ordering the tenders *Flying Fish* and *Sea Gull* to wait ten days for the arrival of the *Relief*.

The two small schooners rode at anchor in Orange Harbor until April 28 and then sailed for Valparaiso. Almost immediately they were struck by a gale which separated them. On the twenty-ninth, the commander of the *Flying Fish* took shelter from the storm in the lee of False Cape Horn—an island frequently mistaken for the Cape itself—and from there he sailed into a small harbor to wait out the gale. When it was over, he set out once more and after an uneventful journey arrived in Valparaiso on May 19, alone.

No person of the expedition, and no member of any other ship sailing those waters ever saw the *Sea Gull* or any trace of her again. She was lost with all hands on that final journey toward safety.

Yet it took little imagination on the part of an experienced seaman to visualize the *Sea Gull's* last hours. The small shallow draft vessel, bucking the growing seas, the wind raging through the rigging as her bow plunged down the flank of a wave and buried itself in the next mountain of water, the foremast snapping, the jib tearing away, the lines fouled on deck and the shouted orders that could no longer be obeyed. Then wallowing, lost in the trough of a great wave, broaching, rolling in one last final spasm before disappearing in the sea of foam and the last shout of a survivor smothered by the noise and the scream of the wind.

Wilkes could easily visualize that and he did, remembering that the *Sea Gull's* foremast had had to undergo repair at Rio. She had not been the soundest of ships to begin with.

The expedition commander sadly wrote the best account he could of the event that no living man had witnessed and then turned his attention to the next voyage of the expedition.

THE United States Exploring Expedition was entering a new phase of its mission and Wilkes set about preparing for it with his customary dispatch. He first ordered all ships of the squadron to Callao from Valparaiso. At that port he ordered the *Relief* to proceed in advance of the squadron to Sydney, Australia, where she was to leave her great store of supplies for the next season's assault on the Antarctic. The *Relief* was then ordered to the United States which would end her participation in the expedition.

Aboard his flagship the *Vincennes* in Callao harbor, Wilkes wrote a lengthy order for all officers and men. The principal point of the message concerned the crew's attitude toward the natives of the various islands of the South Pacific that they would meet.

Wilkes was well aware of the trouble early explorers had encountered and of the death of the English explorer,

James Cook, at the hands of natives of the Sandwich Islands (Hawaiian). This had occurred in 1779 and during the intervening years, whaleships, warships and missionaries of a dozen countries had landed on the many islands of the Marquesas, Samoan, Fiji and other island groups scattered over the wide Pacific. In some cases civilization—as white men knew it—had taken root and the islands were reported to be safe. But in other isolated places, little had occurred to change the native outlook, which in some cases included cannibalism. In still other cases, the outrages of white men inflicted on the natives turned friendly groups into hostile armies. Missionaries themselves, not always as understanding as their instructions indicated they should be, had stirred trouble either from trying to force natives to accept their teaching or by exercising unusual and unjust authority, treating the natives as slaves and inferior beings.

Wilkes knew that the impressions that he and his men made would set a pattern of behavior among natives regarding white men for years to come. In particular he realized and stated that all hands were representatives of the United States Government. An unfavorable meeting with natives of any island could cause death or injury to Americans who followed them.

The primary purpose of Wilkes' voyage among these islands was to survey them, find harbors, ascertain the exact locations and dimensions of as many islands that would offer safe anchorage as possible. Much of the work would entail putting off from the large ships in small boats to set up survey points, measure the height of mountain peaks and determine safe passage through the coral reefs. Inevitably, then, the men would have to come in contact with the natives.

In his order, Wilkes stressed that the men were to treat the natives with kindness and courtesy which, as he pointed out, were "well understood and felt by all classes of mankind." He cautioned against any show of contempt for the customs of the people and informed his men that native ideas of private property did not parallel their own. In short, stealing of white men's property was common and had been the principal cause of friction between whites and natives in years past.

In July of 1839 the four-ship squadron set sail from Callao: *Vincennes, Peacock, Porpoise* and *Flying Fish*. Everyone was filled with a sense of new adventure—and hopefully of a more pleasant time than their recent journeys into the Antarctic had offered.

The first landfall among the islands that Wilkes sought was in the Paumotu group, specifically the Island of Minerva on the eastern edge of that group. Among the many projects Wilkes had in mind was the tracing of the Polynesian anthropology all the way across the Pacific, from island group to island group.

Exactly one month and one day after leaving Callao, the island was sighted and the men crowded the rails and rigging of the vessels to get their first look at a true "South Sea Island." It appeared on the distant horizon like a fleet of ships, according to one report, for the first part of it that was visible was the palm trees. And as the ships sailed toward it, these trees alternately appeared and disappeared as the vessels rose and fell in the long Pacific swells. Then a long white beach became visible with the surf breaking evenly on it. A coral reef encircled a blue, perfectly smooth lagoon and the ships parted company to sail around the island to begin their survey. The results showed the island to be ten miles long by one-and-a-half wide. Yet the highest point of land was only twelve feet above the sea.

Having completed soundings and observations from the sea, Wilkes prepared both scientists and officers with crews to land. It was to be their first encounter with Polynesian natives and they wanted everything to be as pleasant as possible.

Boats were lowered. Several naturalists, the boat crew and officers (Wilkes included) scrambled into the smaller craft. From the level of the rising and falling ocean, the surf appeared to be the greatest obstacle to their landing. Wilkes' boat crew rowed cautiously toward the breakers but he decided the waves were too rough to permit a safe passage. So while the crews held the boats just outside the line of breakers, naturalists and officers jumped into the water and swam ashore.

The naturalists immediately began to search for specimens; Wilkes, walking barefoot through the soft sand, peered into the sparse vegetation for signs of the natives. Finally, at some distance from the group, he located five men and two women. The men were armed with long spears but they would not approach the explorers despite every signal Wilkes made offering them presents. After several hours, the men swam back to the boats and Wilkes watched the natives walk to the water's edge, searching for objects the strange visitors might have dropped. Wilkes again made many gestures indicating that he wanted the natives to come to his boat. Again he was refused.

It began to look as though no trouble could possibly develop since no contact could be made.

Wilkes retreated to his ship for the night but the next day, determined to make some contact and, not at all incidentally to complete the land observations needed for his survey, he returned with crew and officers but this time taking with him an interpreter he had on board. The man was one John Sac, a native New Zealander who could speak Tahitian—a language everyone hoped these reluctant natives could partially understand.

As Wilkes' boat neared the surf again, a group of seventeen natives came to the shore brandishing spears and clubs. Wilkes saw more natives in the undergrowth back of the beach and none looked at all peaceable or friendly. The boat stopped outside the line of breakers again, riding easily in the swells. Wilkes waved a white flag from the bow but the only response he got was more spear waving. He next ordered his Tahitian-speaking crew member to start trying to communicate. John Sac replaced Wilkes in the bow, stood up and shouted. The natives apparently understood him and shouted back. After a few moments Wilkes called for a report. Sac shook his head in disgust, saying that all the natives were saying was "Go to your own land. This belongs to us. We do not want to have anything to do with you."

Wilkes eyed the shore and the surf. The waves were too boisterous for him to order the boat to the beach. And if he, or anyone else, jumped into the water for the short swim to shore they would be unable to defend themselves if attacked. It seemed that the natives' wish to be left alone might be granted by the circumstances. But Wilkes was nothing if not a determined man so he stood in the bow and threw presents toward the beach. The natives grabbed them greedily but still waved their spears and warned the explorers not to land.

John Sac began shouting angrily at the natives. His temper was short and he hated to see the presents being taken with nothing given in return. He stood again in the bow of the boat, waving the boathook just as the natives waved their spears on the shore. He was, in fact, a New Zealand chief himself and in his anger, all the look of a common sailor vanished. What Wilkes and his men saw was a proud native warrior who felt he and his shipmates had been insulted. But whatever his feelings he was not helping Wilkes make contact.

The sound of Sac's voice indicated to Wilkes that he was hurling insults at the natives on shore—who hurled them right back at the outraged New Zealander.

Several other boats from the ships arrived outside the surf and a number of officers asked Wilkes if they might swim ashore. It was the only way, apparently, they were ever going to meet the natives. Although he knew it was dangerous, Wilkes gave his permission but ordered that rifles and pistols were to be left in the boats. Two young officers jumped into the surf and swam to the beach where they were instantly met by natives brandishing spears.

The two adventurers plunged back into the surf and swam to the boat.

Their retreat gave the natives confidence. They stood at the water's edge and shouted more vigorously than ever. An officer called to Wilkes and asked if he could try once more—this time with presents. Wilkes nodded and the man jumped into the surf, his hands filled with gifts. When he reached shallow water he stood up and showed the presents. The native chief waved for him to go back to his boat. But the officer finally crawled ashore on some rocks that jutted into the water. He walked toward the chief, holding beads and ribbons in his outstretched hands. The chief backed away at first but then came at the officer and struck him with his spear. The officer dropped the gifts and retreated into the water. The chief followed him, more out of curiosity than anger. He poked his spear at the white man who swam rapidly back to the boat.

By this time, the natives were sure they had the strangers on the run and their shouts and gestures grew louder and more violent with each passing minute. Wilkes had his men load their rifles with blank ammunition and fire at the islanders. They hooted and threw pieces of coral at the explorers. John Sac interpreted their taunts as phrases calling the white men cowards and daring them to come on shore.

Wilkes next ordered his men to load their rifles with mustard seed and shoot at the legs of the islanders. The sting of these charges made the natives retreat to the undergrowth rubbing their legs and Wilkes at last got several men ashore.

Signal fires of the natives sent smoke high above the cocoanut palms and more than a hundred spear-bearing islanders soon gathered in the bushes.

The expedition members on shore quickly completed their observations and returned to the boats. By sunset of that ignominious day, everyone was safely back aboard ship.

This first contact with the natives of the ocean islands of the Pacific was unquestionably a failure. Although the survey was completed as scheduled, the attempt to gather native tools, clothing and artifacts for anthropological study—an important part of the expedition's mission—had come to absolutely nothing.

Four days after sighting their first south sea island, the men still knew little about an actual island itself. Soundings taken offshore by the vessels in their survey revealed the coral formation of the land as well as the shoals and reefs that could prove hazardous to ships. They all had seen the tranquil lagoon inside the reef. But only from a distance.

On August 16, the ships set sail for the next island, Serle, only 26 miles from Minerva. The ships immediately began their survey of the shoreline and coastal waters of the small dot of land while Lieutenant Alden and a crew of men left their ship in a small boat to try to contact the natives. There were very few on Serle but those that Lieutenant Alden did find were friendly to a fault. As Alden's boat approached the shore, the islanders stood their ground holding spears. The officer stopped the boat before it reached shore, wondering whether the incidents of the first island would be repeated. On seeing that the white man's boat was apparently not trying to land, the chief called a small boy from the undergrowth back of the beach and gave him all the spears which he took away. The natives then jumped into the water and swam to Alden's boat. As it rocked gently in the swells and the grinning natives swam around, the explorers traded trinkets for some of the native ornaments. As the smiling crewmen handed over mirrors and beads, turning to whoever called loudest for attention, eager brown hands reached over the gunwale of the opposite side of the boat and more articles vanished. The islanders swam around the boat, shouting and laughing and occasionally hanging onto the oar blades for a rest—or so the young lieutenant thought. What they actually were doing was picking at the copper metal that protected the blade tips, hoping to tear that loose and get away with it. This first meeting with friendly islanders proved to be an educational experience for the explorers.

As the weeks passed the squadron worked its way westward across the broad Pacific stopping at all islands on their route, making surveys of shoals and harbors. The procedure was always the same. When the next island was sighted and the vessels had approached within a mile or two of its white sand shoreline, the ships diverged and sailed around opposite sides of the island. Sounding lines went down and angles were taken on various parts of the island so its true dimensions and shape could be plotted. Wherever possible, shore parties put off from the ships and the small boats entered shallow harbors and explored the inshore reefs. In some cases natives refused to allow them to land; in others there were no natives and the naturalists collected bird specimens, shells, eggs, coral, and insect and plant life.

The first "civilized" natives Wilkes discovered lived on the island of Raraka. As the squadron's small boats approached the narrow entrance of the lagoon, natives appeared on the shore waving a Tahitian flag to indicate their friendliness. These islanders were dressed in various white men's clothes. Some wore vests over their native clothing. Others wore trousers and some sported hats. As soon as the explorers landed, the reason for the display of civilized friendliness became known. There had been a missionary on the island who had taught the natives some civilized habits.

While Wilkes was pleased to discover the beginnings of civilization on the island, he was dismayed by one aspect of it. Whalers and traders had landed there many years before to replenish supplies and water ship or to trade in native pearls. To pay for such articles from the natives, they gave rum or whiskey. At the time of Wilkes' visit, the chief of the tribe himself was firmly addicted to alcohol. Wilkes, in gesture of friendliness, showed the chief and his wife and daughter all around the *Vincennes* and the chief gave Wilkes a present. The expedition commander accepted it and many trinkets and useful implements were given in return. Wilkes believed he had repaid the chief adequately. When the visit aboard ship was nearly over, the chief complained of feeling sick. He also looked displeased. The interpreter said the bad feeling came from Wilkes' refusing to offer the old man a suitable gift in return for what the native had given. Wilkes puzzled over that for a while since he had literally showered the old man, his wife and his daughter with gifts. But when the interpreter mentioned whiskey, Wilkes understood. He ordered a bottle of diluted whiskey given the chief who instantly felt better and departed smiling and happy.

As island after island was sighted, surveyed and landed upon, the entire expedition began to learn that native acceptance of them depended to a great extent on what their relations had been with white men before. On some islands they were refused completely and could not land. On others the natives appeared friendly at first but on going ashore, the explorers found that the friendliness could quickly turn to anger. On one such occasion, Wilkes was invited to the chief's house for a feast. He landed and left the boat crew to watch boats, oars and everything else they had brought with them. Wilkes ate the native food and tried to be as pleasant as possible but as the evening passed, the natives became more and more familiar with him. Toward midnight he decided it would be best to go back to the ship and, saying good night, rose to leave. The chief and his family decided to walk with him to the shore. And so did a hundred natives.

The chief and his brother reached the shore and climbed into the boat, demanding presents. The other natives were crowding into the boat also and those that could not get in were pressed close around the beached craft, effectively blocking Wilkes. He ordered his men to load rifles and drive all natives from the boat. He also asked the chief to use his authority to tell his men to move away from the boat. But the chief's authority, Wilkes soon discovered, was more ceremonial than real.

The crew managed to make most of the natives retreat from the boat but eight of them refused to budge, including the chief. Wilkes presented each of these men with a fish hook with a great flourish—and told them to get out of the boat and leave.

The simple strategem worked and, breathing more easily, Wilkes and his men returned to the *Vincennes* unharmed.

The Island of Tahiti, famed in song and legend for many years, lies about midway across the South Pacific Ocean, approximately on 147° West Longitude. Presently under

French control, it was ruled, in Wilkes' time, by the natives themselves and several nations had sent consular officers to Papieti (Papeete) in the interests of trade. Missionaries were active on the island and the peaceful natives were struggling to adjust to change that they could not resist. Tahiti was a major goal of the United States Exploring Expedition. For in the harbor at Papieti Wilkes expected to repair his ships, replace worn rigging and canvas and prepare for the long voyage among the western islands of that vast ocean. He also had been ordered to complete an extensive survey of Tahiti itself.

So famous was Tahiti even in those days that all officers and men looked forward to that landfall with growing excitement, yet on seeing the high mountains of the island for the first time, Wilkes confessed to being disappointed. Obviously volcanic in origin, the mountains looked formidable and quite barren. Yet on closer approach, the white beaches and a strip of forested slope began to restore the mental picture he had gained of Tahiti through extensive reading.

When the *Vincennes* and the other ships dropped anchor in the generous harbor, they immediately were surrounded by canoes filled with laughing, shouting natives. The noise of the native voices rose higher and when Wilkes asked through an interpreter who among them was a chief, nearly every hand went up. This odd state of affairs was explained when Wilkes was informed that the natives made quite an income doing laundry for passing ships and that the chiefs had first rights to take in a crew's dirty clothing. In fact the queen herself was taking in laundry which her servants worked on.

Wilkes diplomatically spread the laundry income among as many islanders as he could and then was met by the U. S. Consul with the first complaint the expedition had encountered as representatives of the United States. Consul Blackler presented Wilkes with a list of grievances against the native chiefs. These included statements asserting that a whaleboat belonging to a passing American ship had been stolen and the crew of the boat badly treated; that unjust fines had been imposed on United States seamen; that deserters from a whaleship had not been returned to the ship; and that a promise to provide an office for the U. S. consul had not been fulfilled.

A meeting with the chiefs of Tahiti was arranged and Wilkes, accompanied by an impressively dressed group of officers from the squadron, confronted the equally impressive natives. The grievances were read and the chiefs eventually agreed to make amends for all the complaints.

For several weeks the squadron remained at Tahiti. The survey of that island group was detailed and lengthy and repairs to all ships took up a great deal of time. Wilkes dispatched the *Porpoise* on another westward journey on September 20; the *Vincennes* sailed September 25 to the nearby island of Eimeo, leaving the *Flying Fish* and *Peacock* in the harbor at Papieti. They were not ready to leave until October 10.

At Eimeo, three crewmen of the *Vincennes* succumbed to the lure of that island and deserted ship. Wilkes immediately sent the cooperative natives in pursuit—spurred by the offer of a handsome reward for the deserters' return. The men were no match for the natives who spotted them on the mountain slopes and, laughing, ran them down. The men at first seemed ready to fight with the crude clubs they had managed to form but the natives outnumbered them and jumped from rock to rock with such speed and skill that they knew there was no chance. They retreated to the highest ridge on the island where they were cornered by three natives—in full view of Wilkes aboard his ship.

By the time Wilkes sailed from the Tahitian Islands he and all his officers and crew had become familiar with the rituals and customs of the natives. No longer did they have to worry about how to behave. If the natives were friendly there was one procedure; if they were hesitant, Wilkes tried persuasion; if they were hostile, the ships completed their offshore surveys and proceeded on their way. In many ways the appearance of an uninhabited island was the most welcome sight of all. For then the naturalists found animal life in plenty and there was never a question of spending time bargaining or arguing with the natives. Boats could go ashore unmolested and a wealth of material was gathered for future study.

The Samoan Islands lying to the west of Tahiti were the next major group the expedition planned to survey and to establish sound relations with the Samoans for the future of the United States.

The passage of the *Vincennes* to the island of Opolu in that group was easy and tranquil, but the tranquility ended on the ship's arrival in the harbor of Apia. Here Wilkes found the *Peacock* already swinging with the tide at her anchor.

A message came to Wilkes from Captain Hudson the instant the *Vincennes* let go her anchor and the last sound of the chain died away over the water.

Hudson's message was that he needed Wilkes ashore at once. The expedition commander went overside into a small boat with a premonition that the past few peaceful days were indeed over. He was right.

Captain Hudson had arrived a few days earlier and on going ashore had been told by the natives that one of their tribe had murdered a United States citizen, one Edward Cavanaugh of New Bedford, Massachusetts. Hudson ordered his men to arrest the native and take him aboard ship. He then told the chiefs that a trial must be held and so a gathering of the chiefs (called by them a fono) had been arranged. It took place on November 27 and Captain Hudson had the native, whose name was Tuvai, brought from the ship to the meeting place.

Captain Hudson told the chiefs that Tuvai had to be punished to protect future white visitors to the islands.

The trial took a very short time since everyone on the island knew Tuvai was guilty. But Captain Hudson persuaded the chiefs to ask the prisoner if he had indeed killed Edward Cavanaugh. Tuvai said that he had. Asked why, he responded that he wanted the man's clothes and knife, that was all.

Before the trial, Captain Hudson had told the chiefs that the punishment for the crime of murder was the death penalty and when it became clear to the chiefs that there was nothing to excuse the killing of Cavanaugh they were suddenly aware of what Captain Hudson planned to do.

One of the chiefs rose and argued that it was not the custom in Samoa to put men to death for crimes, that many white men had come to the islands and killed natives without being punished. He argued further that the law of death for murder was unknown to Samoans and he asked Captain Hudson whether the Christian religion sanctioned the taking of human life.

This chief was seconded by another and yet another leader of the native tribes. But when they had finished, Captain Hudson told them that nothing but the death of the prisoner would be just. And he said further that the Samoans must do it themselves.

The chiefs began talking excitedly among themselves, still turning from time to time to Captain Hudson and saying that the Samoans knew no such laws as the white man. They pleaded with Hudson to take Tuvai aboard the *Peacock* and execute him there—or better yet take Tuvai away with them and leave him on some uninhabited island.

It was at this point that the *Vincennes* dropped anchor in Apia and Wilkes was sent for. He conferred for a long time with Hudson. Captain Hudson told Wilkes his plan had been to call for the death of Tuvai and be as harsh about it as possible but then, at the last moment, to reprieve him in hopes of gaining the future goodwill of the Samoans.

Wilkes felt that the man should be taken to some island and left and this was the final course decided upon.

Tuvai went aboard the *Peacock*. The chiefs were informed that he would not be executed but another problem arose. Neither the prisoner nor his family and friends wanted to see him go. Tuvai, in fact, stated he would rather be executed and buried among his native friends than be taken away forever. The chiefs, Tuvai's family and all his friends came aboard the *Peacock* to bid him good-bye. Tears and cries came to Wilkes' ears in such abundance that he quickly saw through the deception. Everyone from the chief, old Pea, on down was trying to soften the punishment and appeal to all the white men's sympathy.

Wilkes knew that if he relented, no decision of any official would ever again be respected, so he refused to change the sentence.

Another criminal, however, was loose on the nearby island of Savaii. His name was Opotuno and he was a chief with his own village and people but with the blood of at least 12 white men on his hands. He had, in fact, declared personal war on all white men and had been such a problem that a United States warship had once been sent to Savaii to arrest him. When any warship appeared off the shores of Savaii, however, Opotuno would take to the hills and remain hidden until the search was given up.

Wilkes discovered that Opotuno was hated by many of his fellow chiefs of other tribes throughout the Samoan Island group and he hoped to get them to help him catch the man.

But on the off chance that his own men could locate the murderer, Wilkes sent Captain Hudson and the *Peacock* to Savaii. Hudson went ashore in a small boat and hiked to Opotuno's village. The chief had left for his mountain hideout. Hudson knew he could not hope to locate the man so he gave up the pursuit and returned to Apia on Upolu.

In another village on that island, Wilkes had met the chiefs and called another meeting or fono. The main purpose of this meeting was to reach agreements with the leaders of the native tribes concerning their treatment of sailors from United States ships who landed on the Samoan Islands. One of the items agreed upon stated that natives who injured or robbed visiting sailors would be turned over to the ship's officers for punishment.

When that agreement was reached, Wilkes surprised everyone by asking that the natives immediately capture

Opotuno and deliver him to the expedition for the crimes everyone acknowledged he had committed.

The strategy failed. The chiefs who were present admitted they hated Opotuno but pointed out that he was a chief and related to other powerful chiefs. His capture by the islanders would touch off a civil war. The chiefs went on to say, however, that they would not stand in the way of sailors from the squadron searching for and capturing the man.

Wilkes knew this was not practical. Captain Hudson had just failed and everyone before him had failed. He knew he could go no further in pushing the natives and he also knew that he had spent far too much time in the Samoan Islands. He was behind schedule.

Before ending the meeting with the chiefs, Wilkes announced a reward for the capture of the offending chief Opotuno dead or alive. It was a trick the other chiefs appreciated. They had never heard of such a thing but it appealed to them. For if only one or two persons captured or killed the criminal, it would not call for a civil war. While if an entire tribe set out, it obviously would bring trouble.

The chief who had presided at the fono was so happy with the idea he said loudly, "Give me the paper—I will put it upon my house where the world shall see it."

The meeting ended and Wilkes returned to the *Vincennes*. It was November 10 and already late in the season. Surveys had been finished and all ships were together again in the harbor. On that day, the squadron set sail for Sydney, Australia. Everyone had had a baptism of fire in the South Seas. They were now ready for a second baptism of ice in the Antarctic.

When the ships left the Samoan Islands they were 19 days away from their next goal: Sydney, Australia. It would be the first civilized port of call since the squadron had left Callao on the west coast of South America. But Wilkes had one more chore to accomplish before making that landfall. The prisoner Tuvai still languished in the hold of the *Vincennes* awaiting his exile on a "deserted isle." Wilkes had told all the island natives that he intended to put Tuvai on a coral atoll where there were no cocoanut trees—to make his punishment seem severe. Actually he had had no intention of that.

Two days after sailing from Savaii, the *Vincennes* sighted Wallis Island, which on close inspection proved to be a closely knit group of nine small islands completely surrounded by a coral reef. The land was high and there were plenty of cocoanut trees in view. As the ship neared this land, a small canoe put out from shore and Wilkes' ship was boarded by a native who spoke a little English.

Here was the opportunity to get rid of the prisoner and Wilkes talked with the native, telling him he was to take Tuvai with all his worldly possessions, put him on Wallis Island and present him to the chief of the tribe.

Wilkes was in a way providing Tuvai with a protector and guide with the hope it would keep the prisoner from being set upon and robbed or killed.

Tuvai was hauled on deck and informed of his fate. He grinned from ear to ear, talked with the Wallis Island native, waved to everyone and left the ship after enthusiastically shaking hands with the sentry stationed at the gangway.

Wilkes immediately set sail and laid a course for Sydney, passing Hoorn Island, Mathews' Rock and Ball's Pyramid, all rocky and forbidding masses of land rising from the sea. At Mathews' Rock the ship paused long enough for two men to swim through the surf and gather a few geological specimens.

Accompanied by the *Peacock,* the *Vincennes* made all speed to Sydney, arriving outside the harbor just as it was growing dark. They had no pilot to guide them into the anchorage but Wilkes was in a hurry and he had been told the charts of the harbor were accurate. Accordingly he took the *Vincennes* into the dark harbor that night anchoring at 10:00 P.M. quietly among ships of commerce. The *Peacock* shortly afterward let go her anchor beside the flagship.

When dawn came, the people of Sydney looked out to find two strange men-of-war riding at anchor. It caused considerable surprise.

VINCENNES IN DISAPPOINTMENT BAY

THE day following the *Vincennes'* arrival, the *Porpoise* and *Flying Fish* reached Sydney. The American consul came out to Wilkes' ship and climbed aboard. He reported that the supply ship, *Relief,* had left but a few days before after depositing all her remaining supplies.

On the morning of his arrival Wilkes went ashore to pay his respects to the Governor of the (then) New South Wales Colony in the city of Sydney. He wore the uniform of a captain in the United States Navy, even though he had not been officially raised to that rank. He left behind him aboard his own ship officers who were nursing grudges against him. They did not like his assumption of rank; nor had they forgotten the extra lashes with the cat-o'-nine-tails Wilkes had ordered for crew members who had been lax during the Pacific cruise just completed.

In addition, one of the surgeons, a Dr. Gilchrist, was extremely angry that morning since Wilkes had refused the man permission to live ashore during their Australian interlude. All of these things, occurring in a kind of fateful sequence, were storing up trouble for Wilkes in the years ahead.

Wilkes' first encounter with the rulers of the Australia colony was stiff and formal. His method of bringing two warships into harbor at night without benefit of a pilot and under the very noses of the authorities did not sit well with the Governor. After all it made the port authorities as well as the military and naval personnel look a little ridiculous. Sensing the coolness toward him, Wilkes explained that he was very much behind schedule and he could not afford to waste so much as a day.

Wilkes' Yankee brashness appealed to the Governor and this, plus his warm manner and not inconsiderable charm, saved the day. The "Aussies" relaxed and offered him and his men all the courtesies of the port. The clubs and homes of the socially prominent citizens became, in effect, second homes for the officers of the squadron.

The crewmen, like sailors the world over, found a welcome in every grog shop along the Sydney waterfront. And Wilkes knew they would. His foreknowledge of this simple fact lay behind his refusal to let Dr. Gilchrist live ashore. For the doctor would be needed aboard ship to minister to the celebrating crew. But the doctor, brooding over Wilkes' refusal to allow him to live ashore, finally lost his temper. He wrote the commander a letter in an outburst of temper and insulted not only Wilkes but the President and the Navy Department as well. When he received the letter, Wilkes gave the doctor twelve hours to apologize. At the end of the allowed time, Wilkes suspended the doctor from his duties.

By this time, many officers of the squadron were at odds with Wilkes. They obeyed orders. They cooperated. But they did not do more. All were trained naval officers and their training and loyalty to the service kept them from actively showing displeasure. But there was little love lost between their commander and themselves.

Wilkes was not unaware of the situation. To him, however, the business of running the squadron did not necessarily include becoming friends with his officers. And he had much more on his mind during the brief stay in Sydney than the attitude of his officers. Once again his ships were in need of repair—and once again the *Peacock* led the list in unseaworthiness.

The *Peacock's* carpenter reported to Captain Hudson that the upper works of the entire ship were rotten. Hudson told Wilkes and added that the carpenter recommended a complete survey of the ship to determine whether or not she could be used further without extensive rebuilding. Wilkes knew he could afford neither the time nor the publicity that such work would receive. He and Hudson quietly looked the ship over and found that the situation was even worse than the carpenter had indicated.

In his report, the man had stated that the shear streak

was rotten in many places as were both berth and gun deck waterways. The gun and spar decks were dangerously worn due to frequent caulking and as a result were very leaky. In his report Captain Hudson added that the shear streak was indeed "perfectly decayed" and that every stanchion on the upper deck bulwarks was either rotten or in an advanced state of decay.

Both Wilkes and Hudson realized the seriousness of the situation. The ships of the squadron had been sent by the government on a job of exploring in high southern latitudes. Any delay, any turning back for lengthy repairs which would make one of the ships miss the Antarctic summer cruising season would bring a storm of criticism when the expedition returned home. That the ships were in bad condition would not serve as an excuse.

Hudson urged Wilkes to let him make repairs on the *Peacock* as best he could and proceed with the squadron, arguing that whatever trouble he got into in the Antarctic would be as nothing compared to the trouble he would find at home if he failed to complete the cruise.

Hudson was a serious and dedicated career naval officer. Whatever public reaction there might be, his training and instinct led him to proceed with a mission and do his best to accomplish it. Consequently Hudson ordered the carpenter to work as rapidly as possible to accomplish as much as time and the situation permitted.

As the days in port passed, more and more interested citizens of Sydney visited the squadron. They could not hide their surprise at the poor condition of the ships. (One gentleman predicted that all ships and men would surely perish in the Antarctic ice.) In particular, they were amazed at the small tender *Flying Fish*. Her two masts and strange rig, her shallow draft, low freeboard and altogether unfit appearance increased the alarm of the Sydney people. It was true that the tender needed repairs; so many in fact, that Wilkes arranged to have entirely new masts stepped, shorter but stronger than the "sticks" she carried.

News already had reached Sydney from England concerning the proposed Antarctic voyage of the famous explorer James Clark Ross and his two ships the *Erebus* and *Terror*. The English Government had commissioned Ross to lead an Antarctic expedition of discovery. Advance reports indicated that his ships were especially strengthened for ice work. They also were reported to have been compartmented below so if ice ripped open the hull, water would not flood the entire ship. In addition, the English expedition was said to have huge ice saws to cut a way out of the frozen Antarctic pack.

Where, asked the good citizens of Sydney, were the American's precautions, provisions, protection against scurvy, ice saws, life-saving equipment?

Wilkes was forced to admit he had none of these things.

There was much shaking of heads among the sea-wise Australians. Disaster surely would strike the American ships.

Wilkes kept repairing his ships, gathering supplies

and making plans for the voyage ahead. Yet even with the most careful planning for the emergency of being frozen in the ice over an entire winter, he could not load enough provisions to assure food and fuel for everyone. And since the principal purpose of the Antarctic voyage was geographical and magnetic exploration, there was no need to take along all the scientists. By mutual consent, the scientists agreed to remain behind in Australia while the squadron sailed south. They would have all the work they could handle studying that small continent's fauna and flora. Aboard one of the ships they would have little to employ their skills and, more importantly, there would be more men who had to be fed, clothed and kept warm.

A farewell Christmas party onshore capped the preparations for the southern cruise. Wilkes decided to give the party as an expression of thanks to the hospitable "Aussies" and from all accounts he succeeded in showing his appreciation to all who attended his sumptuous entertainment.

On December 26, at six in the morning, the squadron set sail to the cheers of well wishers who lined the shores of the harbor. The four ships, sailing in close order, cleared the harbor and a course was set south. It occurred on the exact date planned so many months before in the orders Wilkes received in the United States.

Light winds and fair weather stood ahead for the next six days. During this time the men worked as hard as they had in the harbor at Sydney, for there were many things yet to be done before the cold weather of the high latitudes came on. The crews caulked all decks and hulls, covering the seams with tarred canvas. They built extra hatch covers and doors so weighted that they would not be left open carelessly in the cold climate.

Wilkes paid special attention to the drying stoves that were the sole means of keeping dampness from reducing the men's efficiency. He was not concerned with warmth as much as dryness and in fact planned a 50° temperature for all below-deck areas. He felt that this temperature was sufficient to keep the men healthy—it would in fact encourage activity to generate animal heat—and he had thermometers hung at various places within the ships to keep a check on the temperature. All rigging and sails were inspected and repaired and topgallant masts were shifted.

Shortly after leaving Sydney Harbor, the master-at-arms of the *Vincennes* reported two stowaways had been discovered. Wilkes could do nothing about them except put them on his rolls—for food only until they proved whether or not they deserved to be paid.

Signals and the plan of action of the entire squadron had been thoroughly gone into before the ships sailed. As before, they were to operate in pairs: *Vincennes* and *Porpoise, Peacock* and *Flying Fish*. But Wilkes gave some latitude to each ship commander. The goal of the expedition was to get as far south as possible, for up until that time, no one truly knew what lay behind the ice in high latitudes. Some governments believed ships might be able to sail to the south pole and had so worded their instructions. Land had been sighted at a few points around the shores of what we know today is an entire continent, but in Wilkes' time the Antarctic was a blank space on the map. So Wilkes gave orders to his commanders to keep probing southward. It was the supreme goal.

On January 1, the good weather ended. The wind rose and the waves began buffeting the ships. By midnight, the *Flying Fish* was far from the squadron and Wilkes made signal for her to rejoin. No answer came from the small ship and by morning she had vanished. Fog now obscured the seas although the wind and waves continued. Wilkes ordered both the *Peacock* and *Porpoise* to search for the small tender, for everyone remembered with a chill the vanished *Sea Gull* and her men. The two smaller ships began to sail a pattern east and west of the *Vincennes*. All ships fired cannon as signals and waited for minutes afterward for the sound of reply. But only the wind and the hiss of waves came to the listeners' ears.

Wilkes had no choice but to continue on his mission. He signaled the other ships to rejoin him and the southern probe continued. He cautioned the ship commanders to sail in close order with the *Vincennes* during the night and whenever foggy or stormy weather threatened.

In the event of separation, his orders were for them to sail south and west, for it was his hope to locate an indentation in the ice fringe of the Antarctic as large and deep as the Weddell Sea on the opposite side of the continent.

Shortly after the *Flying Fish* vanished, the *Peacock* also disappeared. This event did not disturb Wilkes unduly. He knew Captain Hudson had to be more cautious with his ship and he therefore ordered the *Vincennes* to continue cruising on her chosen course.

On January 10, the *Vincennes* and *Porpoise* sighted the first iceberg—over a mile long and 180 feet high. As the two ships worked their way southward and westward, the bergs became more frequent. Sailing among them was hazardous. Sea smoke or fog cut visibility to little more than a ship's length much of the time and lookouts strained their eyes for a glimpse of the white cliffs of ice ahead.

Fortunately seas were calm among the giant icebergs, and winds were light. But the ships had to maneuver quickly to pass through lanes of open water. Temperatures now were close to freezing and the moist fog-filled air froze on rigging, sails and decks.

Then from the masthead came the lookout's cry of ice ahead. And by ice he did not mean more icebergs but the edge of the impassable ice pack itself. The *Vincennes* cruised westward along its edge hoping to find a channel for further southing.

Sea elephants lying on the ice and the flitting forms of petrel and Cape pigeons were traditional signs that land was near. The *Vincennes* frequently sailed inside the ice pack in small bays bordered on the south by an apparently limitless barrier of ice stretching as far south as a lookout could see. It was dangerous work, for the sail ships could not maneuver in the small bays as agilely as powered ships of today. There was no way to move astern and they always were at the mercy of a capricious wind.

Throughout the days of watchful sailing men on all ships had reported what appeared on the southern horizon as "the appearance of land." Everyone, Wilkes included, was skeptical of the first reports, for in those latitudes a bank of clouds distorted by mirage could give the appearance of land on the horizon.

From time to time during that period, the *Porpoise* parted company with the *Vincennes* and, on one such occasion, came across the *Peacock* also probing southward and westward along the icy barrier.

On January 16, all ships once again sailed in company and it was on that day that Wilkes admitted that what they indeed were seeing on the southern horizon was land. Observers on the three ships had constantly noted land, the peaks of mountains rising far across the flat ice barrier. Lieutenant Commandant Ringgold of the *Porpoise* was most careful in his observation. He went aloft on that day and saw the dark sloping rise of a mountain peak far across the white ice. Knowing he could easily be fooled by a peculiar lighting of a cloud bank, he remained at his observation post until the sun had radically changed position, but the mountain peak remained unchanged in appearance and position.

Two midshipmen on board the *Peacock* were observing the land at the same time as were lookouts aboard the *Vincennes*. It was the first time that Wilkes allowed himself to state in his record with certainty that land had indeed been sighted.

Knowing as we do today that a whole continent lay south of them, we cannot imagine the excitement this discovery produced. So far as anyone knew, there was no land to the south of the ice fields. French and English explorers were inclined to doubt the existence of an unknown southern continent that had persisted in myth and story for hundreds of years. No chart in existence had laid down any land mass south of the Antarctic Circle and indeed few ships had ever penetrated those ice-strewn waters.

But there was intense excitement aboard the exploring ships. The men did not know the extent of the land but the fact that it existed was as startling to them as it was to the men of Columbus' expedition when he came upon the new world.

Wilkes now decided to let the ships part company and proceed individually on the generally westward course. Alone, each ship could find as much as the three of them together and this would triple the possibility of more land being discovered.

Accordingly on January 17, the *Peacock* set out on her own. For six days she alternately sailed near or lost sight of the other ships of the squadron. On January 23 she sailed into a small open bay in the pack ice near the edge of the barrier. Her lookouts reported land sighted to the south and everyone agreed there was no mistake in the visual identification. But so far, no actual piece of earth had been found, no stone or bit of mud. It was true that the icebergs in their vicinity were much discolored and appeared to have been in contact with land. It also was true that there were many birds and penguins about—which indicate the nearness of land. Several penguin specimens were taken. When they were killed and examined their stomachs were found to contain quantities of pebbles, apparently gathered from the sea floor.

Captain Hudson of the *Peacock* prepared to take soundings in the small ice bay which his ship had entered. Earlier, when the *Vincennes* sighted land, her crew immediately took a sounding but reached no bottom at more than 800 fathoms. Now the *Peacock* tried. Her men rigged a sounding line 1400 fathoms (8400 feet) long and fitted it with several sounding leads. These leads were fashioned so they would trap mud or rock specimens if they touched bottom. They were fastened at different positions on the length of line and let over the side of one of the small boats which had put out from the ship to get a magnetic observation.

The question of soundings along the ice edge was more important than might be imagined. For if any great land mass did lie to the south, the sea floor itself should shoal as the mass was approached. It was the only way—other than by visual observation—that any ship of that time could bring back proof that land indeed existed.

The men in the small boat began to let the line run out and fathom after fathom slipped through their hands without any indication of the bottom lead touching the sea floor. All 1400 fathoms was paid out without success.

Disappointed, the men began taking in the line. They came to the lead that had been fastened at the 500 fathom mark and to their amazement saw a sample of blue and slate-colored mud. They took in the rest of the line and there were samples of mud in all the leads. What had happened then became obvious. Somehow no one had noticed when they had struck bottom and they had gone on paying out the line while it lay coiled on the sea floor. A copper cylinder with a special valve designed to take in a sample of water at great depths finally emerged with the water it contained. The sample was muddy and the cylinder itself was covered with mud.

Excitement grew among the boat crew. They re-rigged the line and rowed a short distance away from their first position. Then carefully lowering the line they sounded the sea floor at 320 fathoms. Another mud sample came up and the boat returned to the ship with the good news. This important sounding supported their visual observation of land in the south.

But it was the last luck the *Peacock* had. On January 24 the pack ice surrounded her and wind began driving her toward a huge iceberg to leeward. The pool of water she was in became smaller and smaller as the trap closed.

Captain Hudson maneuvered his ship desperately. In trying to avoid a head-on collision with a piece of fast-drifting pack ice the stern of the *Peacock* struck another large mass of it. The rudder was thrown to one side and jammed. Then the ice closed in.

All hands manned their stations. A repair crew struggled to free the rudder which was now worse than useless; it was a definite handicap in its jammed position for it would fight the action of any jury rudder they might rig to maneuver ship.

Huge masses of ice now struck the ship from all directions and the wind and current carried the hapless *Peacock* closer to the iceberg whose sheer smooth side towered above the ship's masts. The ice was so close now, Hudson was unable to bring the ship about on another tack. He sent a crew to the ice with ice anchors and lines to save his ship. But just as they were making the lines fast, another blow tore the line from the men's hands. The *Peacock* drove down on the pack ice again, stern first, jamming the rudder still farther over and breaking the braces and pintles that held it in place. For an instant, Hudson believed the entire stern of his ship had been crushed. He furled all sails and used spars as fenders along the water line where the ice threatened to puncture the hull and send the ship to the bottom.

The crew on the ice attached another hawser to the ice anchor and managed to get the line aboard and for a moment the ship seemed safe. But the ice pressed closer around the hull and the wind rose. The fenders took the brunt of the attack by the floes and one by one were ground to splinters by the action. Then the ice anchors let go and the ship was pushed by the floes toward the iceberg itself. She struck the huge ice island on her larboard quarter with a great crash. The spanker boom, the larboard stern davit and the stern boat were carried away in an instant. More and more of the rotten structure of the *Peacock* failed and timbers were started from their frame.

The crew remained at stations throughout the collision and when the ship reacted to the shock, she heeled over to starboard, moving away from the iceberg and into a small pool. Jib and sails were set, yards braced and advantage taken of the wind in that brief moment of respite. The ship had struck the berg near one end of it and with the aid of sails and the increasing wind, Hudson maneuvered his ship away from the immediate danger. But he was still in heavy ice with a storm coming on.

By day's end the ship once more lay caught in the ice. Nothing could be done unless it shifted and in this period of desperate calm, discipline was so well preserved that all hands were served dinner as though they were moored safely in Sydney Harbor.

The plight of the *Peacock* indeed was desperate. The ship had probed a small, narrow bay in the ice barrier and it was there, amid drifting floes and a scattering of large icebergs, that she had run into trouble. To maneuver northward out of the narrow entrance to the bay required favorable winds and enough freedom from ice to work the ship successfully. So far, all Captain Hudson had been able to do was keep his ship afloat and freed from a mortal blow against the towering bergs.

As the evening advanced, the swells running into the bay increased in size, breaking the thick pans of ice and allowing them to rake the beleaguered ship from stem to stern. At every moment, something was carried away with a loud crash: chains, bolts, bobstays, the bowsprit, shrouds. The ice even lifted the anchors which came down after the swell had passed with such force that the eye-bolts and lashings were carried away and the anchors dangled from the stoppers.

The *Peacock* groaned in its battle with the ice. Timbers from keel to deck were wrenched and twisted. And still the swells increased in size and no clear path opened before the beset ship. Hudson ordered Midshipman Eld into a small boat with more ice anchors to attempt that means of gaining control over the ship movements. But Eld and his boat crew suffered in the boat. The ice jammed around it would not permit the use of oars and the men used the oars as boathooks, inching the boat along between the rising and falling pieces of ice.

Under ordinary circumstances only minutes are required for a boat to leave a ship and plant ice anchors, make lines fast and return. In this instance it required two hours merely to get the ice anchors in place and then Midshipman Eld had the problem of returning to the *Peacock*. He and his crew had dragged their boat onto a floe and when lines had been passed and secured, Eld surveyed the situation facing him on the return trip. His only path lay between two icebergs that were dangerously close together. With a great rush the men launched the boat and took their positions. The bergs rose and fell on the swells and the patch between them narrowed as the boat approached it. The men pulled on the oars with all the strength left in them. The boat shot forward and entered the fast-closing channel. But it was too narrow for the extended sweep of the oars. The bergs surged together, squeezing the boat, and the men grabbed oars taking them clear of the ice. Water poured in and in a moment the boat was nearly awash. Then the bergs surged back, letting the boat go for a brief instant. The oars went out and Eld shouted to the men. They gave a few hard, quick strokes and the boat sluggishly moved from the trap. In a few moments, the soaked oarsmen and Eld himself were back aboard the *Peacock*.

But not safe. The wind now came directly against the only escape route for the ship—directly out of the narrow bay. The pool of water in which the *Peacock* lay was so small there was no hope of maneuvering her in the usual manner—nor could the men have done so if the pool had been larger, the rudder still remained jammed to one side. But ice cleared from the *Peacock*'s stern long enough for the men to unship the rudder and bring it on deck. A crew of carpenters immediately fell to work on it.

From eight that evening to midnight, the *Peacock* battled against contrary winds and ice. Working with both sails and the ice anchors, the ship moved slowly toward clear water to north and east of the bay's treacherous entrance.

But for each yard toward safety she gained, it seemed two yards were lost as current and the headwinds drove the ship to leeward where icebergs threatened. The crash of ice under the ship's forefoot sent shivers through every man aboard, for the ship had no extra bracing to withstand the shocks of Antarctic ice. All that night the ship took the beating from the floes and by morning seemed to be in little better position than before.

Examination of the ship's bow revealed the ice was wearing away the thick wooden stem at an alarming rate. Pumps had been manned all night long but water from various leaks continued entering as fast as it could be pumped out.

Clear water still lay to the north but the ice between the ship and the safety of blue water had thickened during the night hours; the swells had broken it into a crushing mass of floes any one of which could crush the hull of the *Peacock*.

Captain Hudson realized only one thing remained to be done—risk everything in one dash to clear seas. By this time the wind had shifted to a more favorable position and he ordered all hands aloft to raise every bit of sail he could carry. The wet, tired crew swarmed up to the yards and loosed sail. The stiff wet ice-coated canvas slowly fell into place. Men on deck braced the yards and the sails cracked and filled with the wind. Then ice began to crash against the weakened stem of the ship. Gaining headway, the *Peacock* began her last desperate struggle to escape. There was nothing the men could do except trim all sail and keep the yards braced to take every advantage of the wind. All were silent as the great floes ground against the bow and thudded against the hull. The din of the crashing floes would have drowned any comment or order that came from the captain in any event. Night came again and the ship still battled the ice. By midnight the clear water was in sight under the round-the-clock daylight of the Antarctic. At 2:00 A.M. on January 26, the *Peacock* broke free.

Captain Hudson set a course due north to safety and sent men to survey the damage to his ship. The carpenters had repaired the rudder for temporary use and stepped it. No great, unstoppable leaks had appeared. But the heavy wooden stem of the *Peacock* had been worn to within an inch and a half of the hull plank ends.

Running clear at last, Captain Hudson consulted with his fellow officers concerning the next course of action. A report on the condition of the ship revealed that she could no longer battle Antarctic ice. Captain Hudson concluded that "After thoroughly turning over in my own mind that state of the ship—with the head of the rudder gone, hanging by two braces, and in such a state that we could hardly hope to make it answer its purposes again, in encountering the boisterous weather we should have to pass through before reaching the first port—the ship considerably strained; her starboard spardeck bulwarks gone as far forward as the gangway; the gripe off, and the stern mutilated; fully satisfied from this state of things that she was perfectly useless for cruising among icebergs, and the accompanying dangers, in thick foggy weather, to which, in these latitudes, we should be more or less subject, and where rapid evolutions are often necessary, in which the rudder must perform its part;

and that the ship would require extensive repairs before being employed in surveying operations; and feeling that the season was rapidly coming around when our services would be required in that duty, I held a council of the ward-room officers, and required their opinions as to making any further attempts to cruise in these latitudes . . .

"There was but one opinion as to the necessity of the ship's returning north, with the exception of Mr. Emmons and Mr. Baldwin, who thought the rudder might stand provided we did not go near the ice or fall in with icebergs. This of course would be to effect little or nothing, and result only in a loss of time. I accordingly put the ship's head north, determined to proceed at once to Sydney, to effect the necessary repairs, so as to be ready at the earliest possible day to join the squadron."

The days of Antarctic sailing for the *Peacock* were over.

Compared with the ill-fated *Peacock,* the *Porpoise* under Lieutenant-Commandant Ringgold had a remarkably safe Antarctic cruise. On January 22, the *Porpoise* lost sight of the *Peacock* and began her own individual journey to the west along the fringes of the ice barrier. Ringgold had instructions to proceed on a generally western course to 105°E Longitude and return. On January 26, a sail was sighted and Ringgold discovered the ship was the

Vincennes. The commander of the *Porpoise* checked his ship's chronometers against those on the flagship of the squadron and bore away to the westward.

Following instructions as closely as weather and ice conditions permitted, Ringgold moved his ship along the barrier following its indentations and promontories as best he could. Always there was a lookout searching southward across the glittering ice for sign of land. Storms frequently obscured the view and when the *Porpoise* came too near the barrier, the very height of it kept the lookout from scanning the southern horizon.

Ringgold was proceeding into totally unknown waters along a dangerous edge of ice which apparently broke from time to time to produce the gigantic icebergs that all the men referred to as ice islands. When he found the barrier tending toward the south, Ringgold did not know whether he actually was rounding a promontory of the barrier or entering a bay. On one occasion he did enter a bay from its eastern opening and soon afterward discovered he had placed his ship in a dangerous position. Wind could trap him in that area amid the hundreds of icebergs and he would have found himself in the *Peacock's* unenviable position. Prudently he sailed eastward and then north to get around the trap.

Land was what the *Porpoise* sought and land was what she found—but not rising above the ice barrier in the form of mountains to be claimed. The land found was mingled with the ice forming the icebergs. Many of them were discolored and had streaks of black or brown earth running through them. Bird and sea life were so abundant that Ringgold knew he was near the land—he simply couldn't see it. While sailing westward along the barrier one day in February, his lookout spotted a black object on an ice floe some distance away. Ringgold hove his ship to and sent a boat crew to examine the oddity. It turned out to be a large mass of black, red and mixed colored earth on a base of snow. Beyond that peculiar appearance of land was another patch of red earth mixed with granite and sandstone.

These bits of evidence—encountered along miles of the ice barrier edge—plus animal life and the discolored water through which the ship sailed convinced Ringgold that land was near. Yet soundings were taken and no bottom found.

On February 14, the *Porpoise* had passed its designated westernmost point. Ringgold had sailed 5° farther west than his instructions called for and found himself on that date at 100°E longitude at a latitude of 64°15′ South. He turned back and began to retrace his course along the barrier, hoping to be able to enter areas which storms on his western journey had prevented him from examining at close quarters.

And although he had encountered severe storms where the barometer dropped as low as 27.5 inches of mercury amid snow and sleet and squalls, his ship was in good condition, tight and dry, and his men were all in good health. As Washington's birthday arrived, Ringgold ordered an extra tot of rum for all hands, called his crew together and congratulated them on their devotion to the expedition and the way in which they had carried out their duties.

On February 24, at Latitude 64°29'S, Longitude 126° East, Ringgold turned the *Porpoise* on a northeastern course and sailed for Auckland Islands. Only one incident had marred his entire cruise.

It had occurred on January 30 late in the afternoon. The *Porpoise* had been sailing in fog and snow and high winds; Ringgold hove his ship to and furled sails waiting for the weather to clear. By midafternoon the visibility increased and he was surprised to discover two ships sailing together some distance away. At first he thought they were the *Peacock* and *Vincennes* but as he approached to signal and speak to them, he saw they were smaller and of a different rig from his companion's ships. Ringgold's next conclusion was that the ships belonged to the English explorer James Clark Ross, reports of whose expedition had reached Wilkes' squadron before it left Sydney and headed south.

Ringgold changed his course and headed for the ships. He was so confident that the ships were of Ross' squadron that he was, as he reported, preparing to cheer the famed discoverer of the north magnetic pole.

When the *Porpoise* came within a mile and a half of the ships, Ringgold broke out his colors showing the flag of the United States as was the custom. The two strange ships broke out, not the English but the French flag. It was then Ringgold realized the ships must be those belonging to the French explorer Dumont D'Urville. He overtook the ships rapidly and was setting a course to pass astern of the Frenchman's flagship. He had got to within musket shot of the French vessels when he noted that they were making sail and, apparently, not going to exchange the customary courtesies of naval vessels. Such an exchange seemed even more appropriate considering the isolated and dangerous latitudes in which the expeditions met.

Quick-tempered Ringgold, believing the French ships were ignoring the United States vessels, hauled down his flag, changed his course and resumed his cruise. Not a word had been exchanged. Later, when Wilkes learned of the odd meeting he was equally furious with the French commander. It was a snub that naval usage could not permit to pass unnoticed. As a result, in his report of the expedition some years later, Wilkes referred to the behavior of the French in tones of anger and bewilderment.

In an even later report by D'Urville himself, the French explorer claimed that he was making sail when sighted by the *Porpoise* for the express purpose of altering course to intercept the United States ship and exchange greetings as well as information. D'Urville claimed that Ringgold mistook his actions but when the *Porpoise* lowered her colors and turned away, D'Urville had no choice but to continue on his way. It was an embarrassing situation all around.

Aboard the *Vincennes*, Wilkes was naturally the most eager of all members of the expedition to discover land to the south. He was convinced that the Antarctic was a continent and by January 22, when the ships parted company for their separate cruises, he and the others had sighted enough distant peaks to assure themselves that a continent indeed lay beyond the ice barrier.

The *Vincennes* followed on the heels of the *Peacock* and passed an indentation that the *Peacock* had found open and had entered. When Wilkes arrived at the same point a day later, he found the bay blocked by ice. Thirty miles west of the position and following the barrier as closely as the great shifting icebergs permitted, he came across a curious group of them clustered around one spot and not moving at all. It was such a curious situation that Wilkes' only conclusion was that they were aground on shoal water, probably a shoal surrounding a submerged rocky isle.

He passed this collection of grounded icebergs and found comparatively clear water to the south in a large bay. Promptly he set a course into it and noted the appearance of land on either side of the bay in a southerly direction. The indentation was about 25 miles wide and Wilkes sailed the *Vincennes* 15 miles south through clear water until ice again blocked his way. He had been so enthused by this apparent passage southward that when ice halted his ship he was bitterly disappointed—so disappointed that on leaving that indentation he named it Disappointment Bay.

A hint of his nervous excitement comes from an incident that occurred the next day. He saw a log entry from the watch officer indicating that when they had reached the southern extremity of the bay previously there had been open water extending southward, eastward and westward from the ship's position. Wilkes was so enraged he turned the *Vincennes* back on its course and once more reentered Disappointment Bay. He sailed to the exact position the ship had occupied when the officer made his log entry and called on him to point out the open water. There was none. Ice extended all around the ship save astern where they had entered the bay.

Following this incident, Wilkes ordered every officer of the deck, on being relieved of his watch, to go to the masthead personally and report the ice conditions to him. He did not want to miss any opportunity to make a southern turn should a bay or indentation be sighted in the barrier of ice that confronted him.

On January 25, the *Vincennes* sailed out of Disappointment Bay once more to continue her westward journey. The weather was clear and the air comparatively mild. Wilkes hove his ship to and sent a watering party to a nearby iceberg. The tanks were filled with ice and during that day the same appearance of land that they had observed the day before was noted through the clear air of the Antarctic, lying far to the south.

Having taken aboard ice for melting down to drinking water, the *Vincennes* sailed north and again turned westward.

It was on the twenty-fifth that Wilkes began to make a unique chart of the positions of the large tabular icebergs with which he and everyone had become familiar. Some of these giant ice islands were three miles long and of tremendous height. They did not move rapidly and Wilkes believed that a chart of their positions would give him—for a brief time at least—opportunity to return over a course or escape from thickening weather by relying on such a chart, just as he would in navigating among ordinary islands.

On the twenty-sixth, the *Vincennes* fell in with the *Porpoise* and sailed in sight of her until the twenty-seventh. Wilkes made every effort to keep as far south as possible and when his lookout reported a line of tabular icebergs, apparently aground to the south, he shifted course and sailed toward them. The *Porpoise* continued in her westerly direction and soon passed from sight. Wilkes conned the *Vincennes* right up to the line of giant bergs and, spotting a passage between two of them, sailed into it.

The tall, smooth glittering sides of the bergs cut the *Porpoise* from view at noon. The *Vincennes* at that time was at 65°54′21″ South Latitude, 142°40′ East Longitude. The magnetic variation (angle between true and magnetic north) was 5°08′ easterly. The *Vincennes* was almost directly north of the long-sought South Magnetic Pole which lay somewhere across the impassable ice that blocked the ship's passage.

January 28 found the ship still probing southward, with Wilkes charting the positions of icebergs. But he now was sailing through a sea almost filled with them. At 9:30 that morning the weather was clear and land was sighted to the south; its bearing was duly noted. There were more than a hundred huge bergs in the ship's vicinity varying from a quarter mile to three miles in length and towering as high and higher than the ship's masts. The *Vincennes* maneuvered between the bergs and for forty miles sailed in good weather through them—still to the south. By 11:00 A.M. land was in plain view but the weather began to thicken and the visibility dropped.

Wilkes took stock of his situation. Unquestionably land lay to the south and he longed for a chance to reach a shore and send a party to solid ground. But without question, also, his ship was in a precarious position. When Wilkes looked at the chart of ice islands at 2:00 o'clock that afternoon he was surprised by the number that had been placed there. He was in the midst of an entire fleet of them. If a storm rose, he knew the dangerous position he was in. For in those latitudes a storm does not necessarily "clear the atmosphere," in fact fog and snow and hail and sleet come almost simultaneously. His lookouts would be unable to see the icebergs in his path and his chart, which required visual identification of the icebergs and their relative positions, would be useless.

A report came to Wilkes that the barometer was falling.

By 5:00 P.M. of that day a gale had begun to form. The wind rose and Wilkes ordered topsails triple-reefed. He was torn between the hope of landing on the continent and the obvious danger to his ship and the entire crew. But with the wind already whistling in the rigging and the lowering clouds, he knew that the safety of his men was his first concern. He ordered the ship about. It was forty miles deep in the great fleet of icebergs.

Wilkes studied the chart of icebergs' positions and noted the last one that had been entered. It was of a peculiar and distinctive shape. If he could locate it and set his course, he would be traveling the path on which he had entered the ice. It was, he was certain, the least cluttered escape route for his ship.

Within a few minutes, his plan was shattered. The iceberg was sighted and identified—but only by sailing the ship dangerously close to its glittering bulk for the visibility now was rapidly dropping.

There was only one alternative plan to be taken: post good lookouts, call all hands to their stations and run for it northward through the storm and the invisible, deadly icebergs.

The gale increased and by 8:00 P.M. the *Vincennes* was running under shortened canvas, every man at his post and all officers alerted. The barometer continued on its ominous downward course.

Through the swirling snowstorm, the lookouts strained to see the ghostly white shape of the bergs. The snow and waves dashing on deck quickly froze, covering everything with an increasing thickness of ice. Helmsmen stood listening to a call of "ice abeam," "ice dead ahead," "off the starboard bow" in time to swing the wheel and change course. More sail was taken in but Wilkes knew he had to keep the ship moving. If he hove to during this night of storm none of them would live until morning. The ship passed between giant icebergs and the roar of the waves breaking against the cliffs was as ominous as surf on a rock.

Midnight came and passed. The men stayed aloft struggling with canvas while crews on deck stood by to brace the yards whenever commands came from Wilkes. Like a chip in a stormy lake, the *Vincennes* rose and fell on the great waves of the storm. Spray dashed into the rigging and promptly froze. All lines were covered with ice and the sails themselves were coated with it. The men aloft were weakening rapidly and early on the morning of January 29, Wilkes called them down. The ice had won. No sail could be trimmed, furled, or reefed so solid had the ice become.

The *Vincennes* drove closer to the crowd of icebergs. Sometimes the masses of white loomed suddenly from the darkened sky seeming to be directly above the ship.

As the ship plunged north, drift ice began to batter her bow. It was broken and tossed by the waves and the towering icebergs. As the hours passed, the storm increased in force and the barometer continued to drop.

Despite the ice, Wilkes had to order the men aloft again to try to shorten sail. The wind tore the stiff sails from the men's hands and one curled over a lee yardarm pinning a man beneath it. He could not move or signal his fellows. In fact, his absence from the crew was not reported for some time and he gradually became weaker waiting for someone to come to his assistance. Word went from forecastle to bridge that a member of the crew sent aloft was missing and Wilkes at last saw the man clinging helplessly to the yard. Lines were rigged immediately and the men once more went aloft. They finally passed a line around the man and lowered him to the deck. His unconscious body was taken below immediately.

Although he was the first casualty, the man was just a step ahead of many of the crew. Petty officers reported that some of the toughest men could no longer man their stations.

Short-handed and under shortened sail, the *Vincennes* sailed onward trying to escape. The cry of a lookout from aloft would set the helmsman in motion, the wheel would spin and the ship turn once more, just in time to avoid a looming ice island. At some time during that night of terror and storm, the cries of the lookouts rose to a chorus: "Ice ahead," "Ice on the weather bow," "On the lee bow and abeam."

The ship had entered a cluster of icebergs so numerous that Wilkes reported, "All hope of escape vanished in a moment."

The ship sailed so close to bergs now that eddy currents of air around their mountainous sides threatened to take the wind from the sails. The waves were tossing the ship, rolling it until the lee guns were under water. But a curious stillness enveloped the *Vincennes*. The icebergs were so numerous and so tall they blocked the sound of the wind and storm raging beyond them. Everyone tensed and waited in the eerie stillness. The ship rushed along into an area of almost certain destruction.

Dead ahead, Wilkes saw two gigantic bergs with a wild pattern of water lashing the narrow space between them. There was no way to turn or stop the ship and the *Vincennes* moved swiftly into the dangerous and narrowing channel. The stillness there was even more complete and every man on deck held his breath waiting for the crash and the crushing of the ship which they all felt was coming at any moment.

Still moving fast, the *Vincennes* moved beside the white ice cliffs and gradually, to everyone's astonishment, the noise of the storm began to increase. It rose, finally, to a roar as the ship moved north and passed from between the two threatening icebergs. They were free. The two giant bergs were on the northern edge of the ice and only wild waves and wind met the ship when she passed them.

Daylight finally came on January 29 to a battered ship and a weary crew. Wilkes saw there still were icebergs around but they were widely spaced and offered little danger. The storm had begun to slack off and he hove the ship to, giving everyone a chance to rest. Men and officers had been at their stations throughout the night.

During the daylight hours of that day, the ship idled in the dying storm and at 4:00 P.M., with the weather rapidly clearing, Wilkes ordered sail set. The men sprang to the yards; the helmsmen spun the wheel and the *Vincennes* took up her course again: south.

Wilkes was not to be frightened off his discovery by one storm. The night of the twenty-ninth, the ship sailed cautiously back over the track it had covered the night before. When morning came on the thirtieth, there was not a cloud in the sky. The sun shone brilliantly and a brisk wind moved the ship toward its goal. Once more they entered the great fleet of icebergs where the water was so smooth now that Wilkes claimed a small sailboat could have navigated safely upon it.

The men looked around at the hundreds of bergs and wondered how they had survived that terrifying night of the gale.

By 8:00 P.M. the *Vincennes* had reached the barrier. Land appeared to the south and across a thick belt of ice, Wilkes saw a channel of clear water. He turned the bow of the *Vincennes* into the pack and rammed his way to the pathway toward his goal.

The ship was entering a wide bay under a brisk wind that threatened again to turn into a full gale. Wilkes decided that should the storm increase he would stay in the clear water and drift with the moving ice. He was confident that the ship would move more rapidly than the floes themselves. For the moment, gaining as close a position to the land as possible was uppermost in his mind. He took the *Vincennes* to within half a mile of the rocky shore. A sounding reached bottom at thirty fathoms (180 feet). Wilkes had indeed found land, land that stretched from that rocky shore south, rising to a height of three thousand feet in a mountain peak which was but one of many strung farther southward sixty miles inland. It was here that Wilkes named the land they all had seen to the south throughout their westward journey. He called it the Antarctic Continent. He named the bay Piner's Bay after his signal quartermaster.

That day the wind increased and Wilkes could not send out a party to claim the shore as was customary. The gale rose and once more the *Vincennes* found herself in trouble. But Wilkes maneuvered the ship skillfully within the clear water of the channel, now drifting, now sailing to a more favorable position, riding out the second gale. For thirty hours, the storm raged and when it had blown itself out, the *Vincennes* was 60 miles from Piner's Bay. Wilkes debated about returning there to make a landing but finally decided against it since he firmly believed that somewhere to the west, along the ice barrier, he would come across another bay and another shore that could be claimed.

When the storm died, another problem faced the expedition commander. He was handed a medical report by two of the ship's doctors stating that although only fifteen of the crew were on the sick list, many others had been so worn by the rough weather and their duty that they soon would not be fit to continue. The doctors believed that only by sailing north to warmer weather could the men recover.

Wilkes asked his wardroom officers for their opinion of the situation: Should the *Vincennes* give up its mission or continue to the limit of the ship's and the men's strength?

The majority of the officers agreed that to sail these waters short-handed was to invite disaster and they suggested a northerly heading. Wilkes deliberated for a long time and then decided that his duty and that of both officers and crew was to go the limit. He accordingly rejected all recommendations and kept a westerly course.

Day after day passed with the *Vincennes* dodging the ice, sticking close to the barrier and sighting more and more land as the ship moved westward. During the first few days of his coasting the continental ice barrier, Wilkes worried about his decision to continue in the face of his doctors' recommendations. The sick list grew from fifteen to twenty, to thirty. But by February 10, the number of sick men began to drop. An extra drying stove had been installed and the men had a chance to dry clothes—wet ones being the chief cause of boils and ulcers breaking out on them and making them useless for handling ship.

By February 21, Wilkes decided to turn northward. The Antarctic night was coming; days were shorter and the increasing hours of darkness made navigation and the sighting of land impossible. In addition, the other exploration of the expedition had to be attended to.

Wilkes was convinced that he indeed had determined a continent, not a series of islands, behind the icy barrier he had come to know so well. He reasoned that the ice barrier itself supported his belief. Had there been islands behind the barrier, the edge of icy cliff that prevented sailing farther south would have been more broken and indented where straits and channels separated the island land masses.

So frequently had Wilkes sighted land—distant mountain ranges, long wavering lines of hills, isolated peaks—that he referred to it either simply as "the land" or "the continent" in his journal.

And so, as he prepared to leave Antarctic waters, the expedition commander felt he had accomplished his mission. He called the crew together and announced they were to sail north. The sailors instantly broke into cheers. For them, the ordeal of ice, dampness, snow, cold and danger was over.

Wilkes congratulated them on their attention to duty and their faithfulness, remarking in his own journal that not a single man had failed to do all and more than had been expected of him.

The *Vincennes* came about and her sails filled with a southerly wind as she headed for Sydney—and safe waters once more.

As the day passed and the weather gradually warmed, the breeze grew pleasanter and the men, thoroughly dry at last, lounged on deck under a warm sun.

Wilkes, pacing the quarterdeck, worried about his other ships. The *Peacock* and *Porpoise* had been sighted at various times early in the Antarctic voyage and he had some confidence in their survival—on the basis of size rather than fitness. But what of the *Flying Fish?* She had not been seen or heard of since January 1 when the first storm broke over the squadron.

In that gale, the *Flying Fish* lost her gaff. Lieutenant Pinkney, her commander, ordered sail to be shortened immediately and the jib stay broke loose which carried away the square-sail yard. Crippled and rolling heavily, the small tender tried to weather the storm. At midnight, Pinkney hove his vessel to, to ride it out. When it finally subsided, a course was set for the first rendezvous point, Macquarie Island. Pinkney sighted the *Peacock* there but the larger ship did not see the *Flying Fish*. From that point, the small ship sailed to Emerald Isle and then south toward the ice.

Days of relatively good weather alternated with storms and by January 16, the ship had encountered the first ice in latitude 61°South. When the *Flying Fish* reached the ice barrier and took up a westward course, neither she nor her crew were in good condition. The ship itself had begun to leak badly. All spaces below deck were thoroughly wet and pumps had to be manned. Four of the ten-man crew were sick and unable to stand watches or help handle ship. As the seas pounded the hull of the light tender, the planks worked more and more. Water rose to the cabin floor and time after time, Pinkney had to take his ship northward to get around the ice and reach less hazardous and stormy waters. What was much worse, however, was the crew's condition. With sail set and a gale coming on there were not enough crew members to shorten sail. The violent winds caught the *Flying Fish* and she rolled and pitched in the great seas opening more leaks in her hull.

Until the fifth of February, the small ship battled the weather, the ice and the sea. By that time the crew had reached the limit of its endurance and the members presented Pinkney with a memorandum asking him to save their lives by turning north. Pinkney asked his other officers for their opinion and they pointed out that with four men sick and others about to become incapacitated, they could not perform their mission and should, therefore, go north. Pinkney himself now lay sick in his bunk. The men's quarters were nearly flooded and the officers shared their space with the crew members in the interests of survival.

Pinkney had little left that he could do but head north. On February 6, the *Flying Fish* set a course northward and on March 9 arrived in a crippled state at the Bay of Islands, New Zealand. The *Porpoise* found her there, and Wilkes eventually learned that she had survived.

The second and last Antarctic phase of the United States Exploring Expedition had come to an end. The badly equipped ships had driven south and west as far as they had been ordered. Much land had been sighted and bits of rock and soil had been taken from icebergs as well as the shoaling sea bottom of a coastline—the shores of what we now know *is* the Antarctic Continent.

Penguins, seals, sea elephants and bird life had been collected. Magnetic observation indicated they had sailed from east to west past the South Magnetic Pole which lay somewhere south of the ice barrier. Winds, tides, currents had been noted. The aurora australis was observed on many a night by members of all ships' companies.

The most important aspect of the voyage of course had been the sighting of land at many points along the 1500 miles of barrier that the ships had traversed. In each instance of a sighting, the officers had taken a bearing and estimated the distance to it. Knowing their own ships' positions they could place the land masses in their approximate positions. But unknown to the officers of the expedition two Antarctic phenomena had been at work all the time, conspiring, it seems, to make all their careful work come under harsh criticism in later years.

The two characteristics were mirage and the unusual clarity of the Antarctic atmosphere. Their effects slipped into many of the otherwise careful observations. For although they could count on the bearing from a ship to a distant peak as being reasonably accurate (and reliance could be placed on a navigator's statement of a ship's position at a given time) no one could trust the "estimated" distance from ship to the sighted land mass. The seeds of Wilkes' oblivion had been planted.

TONGA CANOE

WHEN Wilkes arrived at Sydney, the townspeople flocked aboard the *Vincennes,* congratulating officers and men and taking as much delight in the safe return of the flagship as if the expedition had been one sent out by their own country. Wilkes himself hurried to the *Peacock* to get a report from Captain Hudson. The ship was undergoing extensive repairs in an effort to put her in condition to carry out her duties in the next phase of the expedition.

On first seeing the crippled ship, Wilkes was amazed that Hudson had been able to sail his ship back to Sydney.

She was scarcely fit to sail on a calm sea, much less to weather storms and ice.

The *Vincennes,* too, needed work and three weeks were spent in Sydney restoring the two vessels. At the end of that time, the *Vincennes* set sail, leaving the *Peacock* behind, for she needed even more time to be made sea-worthy again.

Rendezvous for all ships was the Bay of Islands on the northern coast of New Zealand. The scientific men had been there for some time completing their studies of New Zealand (having finished their work in Australia). The *Flying Fish* had gone directly there from the Antarctic as had the *Porpoise.*

The *Flying Fish* was in poor shape when she arrived. Her mainmast had begun working during the last days of sailing and had to be more securely wedged in the step. She was extensively caulked and painted, her rigging was overhauled, and by the time the *Vincennes* arrived, she was as ready as her crew could make her. The *Porpoise* required some work but of all the ships she had suffered least in the Antarctic.

Officers and men had all recovered. Each in his own way was thankful they did not have to face the Antarctic again.

The next task of the United States Exploring Expedition lay in tropical waters among other islands of the vast Pacific. The first they were to sail for was the Island of Tonga, one of a small group known then as the Hapai Islands or the Friendly Isles of Cook. The entire squadron, minus the *Peacock,* sailed from the Bay of Islands on April 6, 1840, and after a good voyage of 16 days arrived at their destination: Tonga. From a distance it was a typical low coral island measuring no more than 60 feet above sea level. The waving palm trees greeted them and the white strips of sand beach beckoned. But unknown to the approaching explorers, they were sailing into a native war.

On landing, after a dangerous passage through the reef and along a narrow channel to the lagoon, Wilkes found that the people of Tonga were friendly and cheerful. He met the missionaries who were trying to civilize the natives and all those he saw at first were converts. They lived and studied under the missionaries' direction and seemed among the most cheerful islanders Wilkes so far had seen.

But the remainder of the natives in the island group—those who had not been converted—were referred to as "The Devil's People" by the converted natives and there was trouble between the two factions. Shortly before Wilkes' ships dropped anchor in the lagoon, the pagan natives had raided the village of the converts and, a day after his arrival, Wilkes found himself among armed, painted natives who brandished clubs, spears and muskets.

Wilkes immediately set about trying to resolve the problems between the two opposing groups and in this effort he tried to enlist the help of the missionaries. But the more he probed the question, the more convinced he became that the missionaries themselves did not want to stop the war that threatened.

Wilkes met with the chiefs of the Christian tribe and got them to agree to a meeting with the "heathen" tribal chiefs. He then sent a native messenger to the heathen tribe to see if their chiefs would agree to a conference. Both sides feared treachery on the part of the other and to assure the heathen chiefs protection, Wilkes moved the *Vincennes* to a nearby island where the meeting was to take place.

Information came to Wilkes from the heathen tribe that assured him the pagan natives truly wanted to settle the difficulties and live in peace. But the Christian group was determined either to convert their pagan fellows or kill them.

Wilkes finally realized he could not settle the question. After much negotiation, the meeting of chiefs did not take place.

Much of the reason for Wilkes' failure in this crisis was due to the leader of the Christian tribe. He was a tall, intelligent native named King George. And while he was, to all outward appearances, searching for a peaceful solution, he was too wily a politician not to understand that he had the power to enforce his will on the unconverted islanders. He called his own council of chiefs and gave directions for the battle.

Watching from the *Vincennes,* Wilkes saw smoke rising from among the palm trees of the island and knew that his efforts had failed completely. Two of the heathen villages were burned, many warriors killed and the remainder of the tribe driven to other nearby islands.

In only one instance while at Tonga was Wilkes able to settle a serious dispute that would have affected future travelers to the island. A British ship, the *Currency Lass,* had arrived in the lagoon at Tonga from the Fiji Islands to the west. Before her arrival, however, a canoe had sailed in from the Fijis bringing news that the British had kidnapped four native women and were holding them on board ship. King George of Tonga took immediate steps. When the British captain sent a party ashore to fill water casks, King George's men captured two of them and held them as hostages, sending word that unless the women were released and a ransom of muskets paid, the men would not be returned.

Wilkes heard of this trouble and investigated it. At first he could learn nothing about the women. There was no sign of them on the ship, but he then learned they were hidden below deck.

Wilkes talked with the British commander and with King George. He knew that unless he settled this problem, no American vessel—or any other for that matter—could come to Tonga and expect a friendly welcome.

Shortly before the expedition sailed from Tonga, Wilkes convinced King George that he was making a mistake. He pointed out that the men King George was holding were not the ones guilty of taking the women from their Fiji Island homes. He also brought word that if the men were released, the women would be placed ashore under his protection. King George agreed and the incident came to a successful end.

Throughout these troublesome days, the survey parties of the *Vincennes* and *Flying Fish* had been busy taking bearings and soundings among all the islands of the group. The *Porpoise* had been dispatched before the squadron arrived at Tonga to search for an island that had been charted but could not be located at or even near its given location.

Everyone aboard the *Vincennes* and *Flying Fish* was eager to leave Tonga and proceed. One of the chief reasons was the mosquito population of those islands. The insects swarmed over the men and almost put a stop to their observations and measurements. Night work—when the mosquitoes were out in force—was seriously restricted. No one could stand motionless long enough to take an observation. To escape the insects, and try to get some rest, the men took to sleeping in the rigging far above deck—but with little success. Below decks it was impossible. The incessant hum of mosquitoes gave the *Vincennes* the nickname of "the music box."

On May 1, 1840, to everyone's relief, orders came to make sail and weigh anchor. But no sooner had Wilkes given the order than the *Porpoise* appeared outside the reef—and within hours the *Peacock* hove in sight. It was a happy reunion for Wilkes. He had all his ships together and fit for the heavy work of surveying the Fiji Islands—his next objective.

FIJI DRUMMER

THE Fiji Islands (or Feejee as the word was spelled when Wilkes sailed) contained the least-civilized natives in the entire Pacific. Missionary efforts had brought few results and the islanders, savage and warlike, had the added drawback of being practicing cannibals as well.

Throughout the squadron's prolonged stay in that island group, Wilkes constantly bore these facts in mind. Unfortunately, several of his junior officers did not and the result was tragedy.

The Fiji natives, living in small groups of huts near their cocoanut and breadfruit trees, had the usual intricate system of gods, tabus, punishments and rewards of most of the Pacific Island natives. They also had several customs not shared by other islanders. One of the most perplexing of them, so far as Wilkes was concerned, was their outlook on death. They believed wholeheartedly in an after life. So strong had the belief gripped them that fear of physical death was removed and they sometimes asked to be put to death if they felt they had been humiliated or mistreated by their fellows.

The method of accomplishing this was unique. If a person had decided, for one reason or another, that the time had come for him to die, he asked that a funeral be arranged. When that had been done and the procession had started, the person to be killed walked along with his family and friends, talking and laughing. The person then cheerfully entered the dug grave and sat down. A rope or vine was wrapped once around his neck and then those who were to perform the act stepped forward: the person's children.

When Wilkes once witnessed such a murder, as he called it, he was properly horrified. But he was assured by the few white residents on the islands that such acts were the custom. In fact, they told him, when a husband dies, his wife frequently asks to be buried with him, and the wish is always granted. When one chief died, his five wives and daughter cheerfully consented to their own deaths.

Yet as the squadron approached the main group of islands their appearance—green, mountainous, white-beached and beautiful—made Wilkes wonder whether all the stories of savagery were true. The Fiji Islands looked like most people's dream of tropical paradise.

En route to his principal goal of the island of Ovolau, where the already charted and safe harbor of Levuka was situated, Wilkes sent the *Porpoise* on an independent mission. Captain Ringgold was ordered to survey and chart the shoals and reefs on the eastern edge of the Fijis. Thus only three ships entered the narrow channel leading from the sea to the security of the lagoon. When they dropped anchor, Wilkes stared at the natives on the shore and saw a small boat with a white man in it approaching his ship. The man turned out to be one of a dozen or more whites who had abandoned civilization and decided to spend their lives on the island. This one's name was David Whippy.

He had jumped ship 18 years before and taken a native wife. Ovolau was his home. Wilkes found him to be as trustworthy as his reputation indicated. He proved to be a great help since he had risen in the islanders' estimation and was considered to be what they termed a royal messenger or Maticum Ambu.

David Whippy went ashore after greeting Wilkes and brought the chief of Levuka back with him. Wilkes offered the usual presents, trying to establish friendly relations with the none-too-gentle group of islanders. He succeeded and, with Whippy's help, it seemed that he and his men would be able to accomplish their survey which was to be long and tedious among the many islands of the group, without hindrance from natives.

Taking advantage of the chief's welcome, Wilkes immediately organized the first shore party to begin his survey. Wilkes himself, accompanied by about twenty-five scientists, officers and crewmen, began the ascent of Andulong, one of the highest mountains on the island. The climb was more rugged than anyone had supposed it would be, but Wilkes and most of the party struggled with their surveying equipment up the steep slopes, through the shadowed ravines and across hundreds of small streams. Whippy accompanied the group and several native guides preceded the party. Wilkes noticed at one point that the natives stopped, pulled a leaf from a nearby tree and threw it on the ground. He asked Whippy what the purpose was and was told that it was a ritual. A man, Whippy said, had been clubbed on that spot. The leaf thrown to the ground was a mark of respect for the fallen warrior—and if the respect were not given, those who ignored the ritual would soon die themselves. Wilkes remarked in his report of the journey that "judging from the number of places in which these atonements were made, many victims have suffered in this way."

When at last the party emerged on the peak, the entire island lay in view below and around them. The ships rode at anchor, like toys, in the blue mirror of the lagoon. The surveyors had an unobstructed view all around the compass and they immediately set up transits and began measuring angles.

Other islands—as much as 60 miles away—were visible from where Wilkes stood and he could see the extended coral reefs stretching out from the island, marked with a line of white where the waves broke on them.

The men set up the barometer and took readings which, when compared with the matched barometer aboard ship would give them the altitude of the summit of Andulong. Before leaving the ship, Wilkes had given orders to fire a cannon on a visual signal from the mountaintop. When this was done, the time between the flash of the cannon and the sound of the firing would give them data to calculate exactly how far away the ship was, and supply one more measurement needed for the extensive survey they were undertaking.

The return to the ships was as difficult a journey as the ascent. The surveyors slipped and stumbled down the steep sides of the mountain. They ran into the volcanic rock, scratching and cutting themselves. Wilkes wryly admitted that neither he nor his men looked like intrepid explorers on their return. The natives—and the white men who lived on the island—skipped nimbly down the trail, agile as goats. Darkness came before they reached shore and the natives obligingly brought cocoanut frond torches to light the rest of the way.

This first survey journey was only the beginning of far more extensive work on the part of the expedition. The reefs and shoals that Wilkes had seen from the peak—both around the island of Tonga and the adjoining islands—were to be charted. The work required that launches and cutters sail or row along the shorelines, taking soundings and measurements to chart the reefs.

And it was in this work that Wilkes realized danger threatened.

The apparent goodwill of the natives they had encountered did nothing to change Wilkes' opinion of the savage, cannibalistic and warlike nature of the islanders. On the arrival of the *Vincennes*, as a matter of fact, everyone was given an introduction to the true nature of the natives.

In the lagoon into which the *Vincennes* sailed, there lay a small sloop, the tender of a trading ship that had been sailing among the islands of the Fiji group. Her master reported that one of the trading ship's crew had been enticed ashore on an island. He had gone into the undergrowth with the apparently friendly natives, hoping to trade profitably with them. He never returned. The ship's captain and the whites who had made their home on Tonga could easily visualize what had happened. A few steps beyond the innocent white beach, under the shadow of the trees, the man had been murdered and his body devoured by the smiling cannibals.

Wilkes was alerted to the danger involved in sending out his launches and cutters. Scientists were to accompany the young, energetic officers who commanded the boat crews. Many of the scientists were so intent on pursuing their researches that they frequently took extraordinary chances with the natives. The young officers—lacking mature judgment—also tended to believe they were invincible and could "beat anybody, any time, anywhere." Wilkes knew otherwise.

Before dispatching his surveying groups, the commander of the expedition issued strict orders—the strictest orders so far given—in great detail as to how his junior officers were to conduct their boats and themselves.

In particular he ordered:

1) You will avoid landing anywhere on the main land or islands unless the latter should be uninhabited.
2) Every precaution must be observed in treating with these natives, and no native must be suffered to come alongside or near your boats, without your boarding nets being up; all trading must be carried on over the stern of your boat, and your arms and howitzers ready to repel attack.
3) You will avoid any disputes with them, and never be off your guard or free from suspicion; they are in no case to be trusted.
4) Your two boats must never be separated at night, but anchored as close together as possible.

Wilkes dispatched the *Peacock* and *Flying Fish* to other islands of the Fiji group to carry out surveying there. The *Porpoise* was away among the eastern Fijis and as the days passed, the work progressed without incident. May and June faded into July and July found the squadron working more closely together. The *Porpoise* had rejoined the *Vincennes*. The *Peacock* and *Flying Fish* made frequent contact with the flagship. It began to look as though the expedition would complete the survey and leave unscathed.

Wilkes, at this time, had transferred to the shallow draft *Flying Fish* and by July 24 was completing the final phase of the work. A small sand island off one of the larger land masses attracted his attention and he set a course for it. He named the islet Linthicum after his coxswain and when the *Flying Fish* dropped anchor, the men prepared to chart its position with reference to the nearby larger island using triangulation methods. Wilkes himself went ashore with the survey party and assisted in the work. When it was completed, he believed that at last the survey of the Fijis was over. While he and the others were packing the instruments and preparing to return to the tender, he was notified that three small boats were approaching from the Island of Malolo—five miles east of Linthicum Island.

Wilkes hurried back to the *Flying Fish* and, taking his glass, leveled it on the boats. What he saw sent a chill of fear through him. They were the two boats from the *Vincennes* and the one from the *Peacock*. They moved slowly through the water and their flags were at half mast and had been turned "union down" in the universal signal of mourning and distress.

White-faced, Wilkes leaned over the rail of the *Flying Fish* when the boats drew alongside. Stretched out in one of them were the stripped bodies of two officers: Lieutenant Underwood and Wilkes' own nephew, Midshipman Henry.

The commander of the launch, Lieutenant Alden, looked up at Wilkes and called the news. Murder had been committed. The parties had been attacked. What Wilkes had dreaded all the anxious weeks finally had become reality.

Lieutenant Alden, in charge of the party, had read the instructions from Wilkes as had Lieutenant Underwood and Midshipman Wilkes Henry. Henry was a bold, adventurous young man who already had got into trouble with his commanding officer because of his recklessness. Only the intervention of Wilkes had saved him from being sent home. Lieutenant Underwood, an able man, had become intensely interested in learning the languages of the various island tribes. He had developed into something of a linguist by the time the expedition reached the Fijis. And he also had made up his mind that his own friendly spirit could overcome the savagery of the natives.

The launch and cutter under the command of Lieutenant Alden anchored off the eastern shore of the island of Malolo on the evening of July 3. Alden's orders had been that on completion of his survey he would either rejoin the *Porpoise* or the *Flying Fish* until the *Vincennes* and *Peacock* returned from their work.

According to plan, the *Porpoise* was to anchor on the western side of Malolo when she was through and on that evening Lieutenant Alden sent Lieutenant Underwood and one man ashore to climb a hill and see if the *Porpoise* had arrived.

Shortly after Underwood disappeared among the trees Alden noticed natives grouping on the shore. To him they appeared suspicious and he hoisted the recall signal to alert Underwood.

Alden had warned Underwood to go well armed and on his guard but as the moments passed and no one emerged from the trees, Alden's tension increased. Finally, Underwood came from the undergrowth accompanied by his companion and, to Alden's surprise, a native boy. The three returned to the launch and Underwood reported that the *Porpoise* was nowhere in sight. He also explained the presence of the boy.

While returning to the shore, Underwood had surprised the youngster who was hurrying through the forest carrying an armload of warclubs. On seeing the officer, the boy dropped the clubs and began to run but Underwood caught him and forced him to return with him to the boat. It was Underwood's idea that the boy would serve as a hostage for the entire survey party so that if anyone were detained on shore by the natives, the crew would have some bargaining power.

The crew spent the night aboard the boats and on the morning of July 24, another boat joined them, that of Lieutenant Emmons of the *Peacock*. All boats were low on provisions, and after a meager breakfast Alden and Emmons decided to try to trade for some food with the natives who were on the shore watching them. For reasons Alden never learned, the natives refused to trade food for anything. But after several hours of useless talk, one of the older natives waded out and said that someone must go to the village and trade with the chief. Word arrived that the chief had four hogs he was willing to give the men as presents if they would send someone after them.

More bewildered than alarmed at that moment, Alden gave Underwood permission to go into the village and that officer went cheerfully, still firm in his belief that his frank, open manner would influence the natives.

He started for the shore with his boat which was of shallower draft than the launch, confident that Alden would push closer to shore when the tide rose and permit his boat to float over the coral reef that blocked his way. But even Underwood's boat had difficulty and on seeing the trouble, several natives came out to help drag it over the reef. While lending this helping hand the natives saw how few weapons Underwood and his crew possessed. For the cheerful lieutenant had carried only three muskets from his ship even though he had been issued ten.

While this was going on, Lieutenant Emmons landed with his boat crew and went up a small hill to get some final angles for his survey. He saw the eagerness of the natives to reach his boat and he gave strict orders not to allow them to approach. When he returned he stayed in the shallow water near shore awaiting Underwood's return.

Underwood meanwhile had landed and started toward

the village accompanied by John Sac who was to help as guard and interpreter. His own crew remained in his boat. Underwood shortly returned with the news that there were only two hogs and they were not a gift—they were for sale and the only price was musket, powder and ball. This Wilkes had forbidden. Underwood continued to argue with the natives on the beach and then sent a crewman, Jerome Clark, out to Alden's boat beyond the reef to say that for the gift of a hatchet, they could get the hogs. Alden gave Clark the hatchet and a message for Underwood to get off the island as fast as he could.

The tide was rising and as soon as Alden and Emmons could force their boats over the reef, they started toward land. Several natives waded out, ostensibly to assist the crews. But one of them said something in his native tongue to the hostage. The boy's attitude changed and became tense and watchful. The natives helped push the boats forward in the shallow water but then left and returned to the shore. Both the boats lay in about two and a half feet of water and as Lieutenants Alden and Emmons were talking the situation over and waiting anxiously for Underwood to bring his boat and crew to safety, the hostage leaped over the gunwale and started wading as fast as he could toward shore.

Alden aimed his musket at the boy—who was the son of the chief—and called for him to stop. The boy glanced back, a frightened expression on his face, then ducked and headed away from the shore party of his tribesmen and Underwood's boat crew. Instead of stopping he tried to run faster in the shallow water. Alden told his men to fire over the boy's head. The volley rang out over the still lagoon, the shot falling harmlessly in the water beyond the runaway.

Alden ordered Lieutenant Emmons to go after the boy and bring him back dead or alive. On hearing that order, Midshipman Clark raised his musket again and shot the boy just as he reached the shore. The young chieftain fell on the edge of the water and did not move.

His father, the chief, ordered his men to attack. Underwood and his crew had not noticed the runaway hostage but the cry of the savage chief told them that all talk and bargaining was at an end. The instant the chief gave the order, two natives grabbed crewman Jerome Clark's musket and tried to take it away from him. Clark stabbed one of them in the chest with a knife. Underwood hit the other on the head with the butt of his pistol—and then gave the order to his men to close ranks, and back toward their boat in a desperate effort to get away from the island. Without turning his head, Underwood called to Midshipman Henry who was guarding the boat and told him to cover their retreat. Henry answered that he had just been hit by a native and would take care of him first. He chased the native and killed him with his knife. Henry started back for the boat and had just reached it when a native hit him with a club on the back of his head. As he went down, he shot the man through the heart.

On seeing the wounded midshipman fall, the natives

swarmed over him, using their short heavy clubs and Henry was dead.

The men slowly retreated toward the boat, firing their muskets and pistols as they went. More and more armed natives swarmed out of the undergrowth. Some tried to cut off the explorers' retreat by getting between them and the boat. A spear wounded Underwood but he fought on, calling encouragement to his men. Then a club struck him on the head and he fell. Like Henry, he was immediately killed.

Jerome Clark was wounded. He fell unconscious and his friends dragged him the remaining few steps to the boat.

Scarcely a minute had passed since the chief had given his order to attack. The men were dazed and bewildered. Their officers were dead. The natives were crowding around them.

Offshore, Alden and Emmons in their boats were urging their crews forward to rescue Underwood's men. As they reached shore, the men of the other two cutters began firing. They jumped out and started toward the beach, covering the men already fighting with the Fijis. As their firing increased, the Fijis began to run toward the sheltering mangrove trees but they dragged the stripped bodies of Underwood and Henry with them.

Knowing the natives' cannibalistic appetites, Alden urged his men forward. They ran, firing as they did, into the jungle where the bodies of the officers were found.

The dead and wounded were quickly placed aboard the

boats and Alden ordered all possible speed in returning to the *Flying Fish*.

When he saw the murdered men, Wilkes and all the crew aboard the tender were sickened and angered by the sight. Jerome Clark, who was seriously wounded, was taken carefully aboard the tender and doctors worked over him.

Wilkes immediately made sail and then called for reports of the tragedy from Alden and everyone else who had been involved.

Why had Alden allowed Underwood to land? Why had Underwood not taken all his arms in his boat? Why had the young men not followed orders?

There were no satisfactory explanations. But the problem was past explanation anyway. The dead were dead.

Two things were uppermost in Wilkes' mind when the bodies of the officers came aboard. One was grief at the loss of them, a particular grief for Wilkes since Henry was the only child of his sister. The other was: How to discipline the natives so they would not attack visitors again?

All his officers—in the heat of anger—favored landing and wiping out the offending tribe. For them, an eye for an eye was the only policy. But Wilkes refused to be drawn into the natural desire for swift and complete revenge. Yet he knew that the guilty parties had to be punished and while the sad task of burying Underwood and Henry was being carried out, Wilkes turned the entire matter of punishment of the Fijis over in his mind.

To bury his dead, Wilkes at first thought of the sea. There, at least, the natives could not penetrate to seize and desecrate the bodies of the officers. But he also had noticed the number of small sand islands off the shores of the main island of Malolo. These islets, really, had coconut palms and some of the usual jungle undergrowth so he decided to select one for the graves of the two men. To keep the natives from discovering the graves was his greatest concern. He sent the small cutters to patrol the shores of Malolo and keep natives from spying on them from their canoes. Then he went to the seaward side of one of the small islands in the ship, launched one of its boats and took the bodies of Underwood and Henry ashore accompanied by only a few men. Graves had been dug the night before. And after the burial service had been read and three volleys fired over the bodies of the naval officers, the graves were filled. To avoid discovery, underbrush was spread over the unmarked spot and all traces of footprints swept clear from the white sand of the beach. Wilkes named the group of small islands in which they were at the time the Underwood Group. The island on which the graves had been dug was named Henry Island.

The anger of all officers and men of the expedition remained high. All knew that Wilkes would order punishment for the natives and their own desires for revenge were swaying their thinking. Nearly every officer wanted to land on Malolo and wipe out the inhabitants completely. Again Wilkes took a more reasonable approach. He was at least as angry as any officer on the expedition but he knew that excessive revenge in the name of punishment would do more harm than good. People in Washington would not understand it. More to the point, when news of it spread within the Fiji Island Group, such excessive action could cause more trouble for visiting ships and crews in the future. What Wilkes needed was punishment of just the correct amount.

Two towns were located on the island, Arro on the northeast side and Sualib on the southwest. The attack which resulted in the murders had been committed principally by natives of the town of Sualib. Wilkes decided to burn the village of Arro and to attack and burn the village of Sualib. In the planned attack, only women and children were to be spared.

He also wanted to prevent the escape of natives to other islands in their canoes and so he, with several small cutters and an armed force, patrolled the waters and maneuvered into position to burn the village of Arro. While patrolling the coast, Wilkes saw several canoes loaded with natives apparently fleeing to the nearby island of Malolo lailai to the south. His men bore down on them. An interpreter called to the islanders to learn whether or not they were natives of Malolo. When he was told they were—and had relayed the information to Wilkes' boats—his men immediately opened fire. Then Wilkes' boat caught up to the others and he ordered the firing to stop. But the natives already had abandoned their canoes and were swimming for the safety of the shore. One by one they were hauled out of the water. Among them Wilkes found several women and children. These he swiftly put ashore. The men—some of whom had been wounded—he sent under heavy guard back to the ships where they were placed in irons.

With his fleet of small boats he headed to Arro on the northern coast of the island. It was deserted. In addition everything movable had been spirited away overnight and Wilkes knew then that the villagers expected to be punished. He looked beyond Arro up to the high mountain peaks of the island where he could see, here and there on the rocky paths, natives climbing to safety away from the shore, out of reach of the guns.

One by one the huts of Arro were set afire and the plumes of smoke rising above the cocoanut palms told every islander who saw them that the punishment had begun.

Lieutenant Commandant Ringgold of the *Porpoise* had been placed in command of the party Wilkes had ordered to attack Sualib. He had sixty armed men under him and he divided his force into three groups or divisions. He led one. Lieutenants Johnson and Maury led the others.

Ringgold landed his forces and started toward Sualib which lay several miles inland. As the groups approached the settlement, they could hear the Fijis shouting from behind their strong, barricaded walls. Never in the history of the tribe had anyone been able to penetrate the town's fortifications and this gave the Fijis confidence. Wilkes himself admitted later that the tribe had done a good job in fortifying their village. A moat lay around the outside of the walled enclosure. The wall itself was made of coconut-palm trunks interlaced with a thick wicker wall ten feet high, and beyond the wall lay a trench protected by an earthen parapet from which defenders fired on attackers in comparative safety. Gates were narrow and well guarded by a baffle of wickerwork walls through which anyone entering had to twist and turn, exposing himself to the warriors within.

Ringgold studied the fortified town and listened to the chanting of the natives inside the walls. It did not appear that he would have to worry about making contact with the enemy. They were confident of their ability to protect themselves and when Ringgold's force got within bow-shot of the town, the islanders came out defiantly and began shooting at the advancing party of explorers.

Ringgold's men opened fire and Ringgold sent a flaming rocket whizzing among the defenders. The rocket frightened them and they retreated through the narrow gate.

Ringgold gave the order to advance and when his men approached within about seventy feet of the village wall, the Fijis began fighting in earnest. The showers of arrows grew thicker as the women and children of the village joined in the fight. The natives had a few muskets and these they fired clumsily and without effect.

Ringgold and his officers were amazed by one feat of the natives about which the explorers had heard but which they did not believe. The Fijis watched the white men's muskets pointed in their direction and when they saw the flash of the powder, dodged quickly one way or another so as to avoid the musket ball. During the storming of Sualib, many natives escaped injury or death by displaying this astonishing agility.

The battle grew in intensity until, as one officer reported, there was nothing but a general melee. The natives shouted to the white men to "come on;" the muskets blazed away; arrows and spears flew thicker than before.

Ringgold tried again and again to send a rocket into the town to set it on fire but for some reason the rockets failed to work. One finally struck the thatched roof of a hut which began to burn furiously. A young warrior leaped to the roof to put out the fire and one of Ringgold's men killed him instantly with a musket ball.

The fire and the constant hail of musket balls began to discourage the islanders, and, from higher ground away from the village, Ringgold's observers saw the warriors one by one begin to flee through a gate at the rear of the village which had been left unguarded.

By this time the entire village was burning. A number of Ringgold's officers urged him to let them storm the main gate and force their way into the village. But Ringgold decided against it. Had they tried to force their way through the gate, unquestionably several of the attacking party would have been seriously wounded or killed. Ringgold reasoned that enough of the warriors had been killed to teach the natives the lesson Wilkes wanted taught, and that the last task remaining was to level the town and the food plantations by burning them.

The village itself was burning now and Ringgold

ordered his men to move back from the town. The heat was intolerable as more dried, thatched roofs burst into flame, the bamboo walls and frames began exploding like small cannon. The few natives left in the village shouted, women and children screamed, and then the heat and noise and smoke forced all of them to flee, giving up the fight entirely.

On planning the campaign against the natives Wilkes ordered one of Ringgold's three groups to return to the ship after his attack with whatever wounded the battle had produced. As it turned out there was very little damage to the attacking forces. Several men had been slightly wounded by arrows but only one was unable to continue with the main force. Following orders, however, Ringgold dispatched Lieutenant Maury's group to the *Porpoise* with the slightly wounded men along the beach while the other two groups proceeded over the hills toward the town of Arro to link forces with Wilkes and Lieutenant Alden.

There, Ringgold and Wilkes surveyed the results of the punishing attack. Arro had been burned. Many of the warriors of the town of Sualib had been killed and the town and its plantations destroyed. No serious casualties had been suffered by the expedition forces.

Wilkes retired with his men to the ships, leaving the natives overnight to think matters over. In all his actions, Wilkes had kept firmly in mind the guiding principle of the expedition: to make the islands safe for ships of United States' commercial interests. This, in Wilkes' view, meant not only physically safe from uncharted reefs and shoals but also safe from unprovoked attack by the cannibal natives of Fijis and other islands. His decision to attack and kill the armed warriors of Sualib rather than simply burn their village came after lengthy discussion with his officers. Wilkes believed that merely burning the village (which could be rebuilt in a few days by the natives) was not sufficient punishment for taking the lives of United States representatives. It should make no lasting impression on the warriors and certainly, in later years, would do little to prevent further attacks on traders or sailors.

Yet with all his caution and exercise of sound judgment, Wilkes was later to be called to account for his "extremely cruel" actions in the Fiji Islands.

Aboard the *Vincennes* that night, Wilkes waited, hoping for some indication from the islanders that they had had enough. When daylight came he saw a group of older men and several women gathered on the shore. Immediately, he took an interpreter in his launch and proceeded shoreward. As his boat drew near, all the natives save one left the shore and disappeared in the bushes. The person left was a young woman. On the ground about her feet were the pieces of clothing and equipment belonging to Lieutenant Underwood and Midshipman Henry. In her arms she held a live white rooster.

Through the interpreter she said that she was returning the clothing and effects of the two murdered officers and was also giving Wilkes the white rooster. Suspecting that this gift was a symbolic peace offering, Wilkes refused it. Men of his boat crew gathered up the effects of the dead officers and put them in the boat.

Wilkes told the woman to take a message to her chiefs. Tell them, Wilkes said, that everyone must beg the pardon and mercy of the expedition on their knees on a hill where all his warriors would gather for the ceremony—a ceremony, Wilkes knew, without which the Fiji islanders would never admit they were conquered.

Several days passed while messages flew back and forth between Wilkes and the island chieftains. They expressed regret, sorrow, pity. What they did not express was their willingness to beg the pardon of the expedition.

On board the *Vincennes,* Wilkes had the chief of the town of Arro held prisoner. In addition there were several warriors of both Sualib and Arro in irons below deck. Wilkes brought the Arro chief to his cabin and asked a rather startling question. Was there, Wilkes wanted to know, anyone among the prisoners on board whom he would trust with his life? The old chief blinked in astonishment and thought a while. Then he nodded. There were two young boys, fifteen and seventeen years old, who were related to him. They could be trusted.

Wilkes nodded and then told the chief why he had asked. These two boys were going to take a message to the islanders on shore. The message was easy to understand and should give little trouble. But it had to be understood and delivered by the two boys without fail or great trouble would come to not only the chief of Arro but everyone else.

Wilkes' message was this: All the people on the island of Malolo will assemble at the appointed place (the hill Wilkes had pointed out to the young native woman). They would be there when the sun was overhead, that day. They would come to the hill on their knees as was their custom when they were conquered by an enemy.

And what, the old chief wanted to know, would happen if the people on the island refused?

Wilkes told the men that he and all his people on the island would be killed. For Wilkes knew that unless the islanders surrendered according to their own custom, unless they admitted being conquered in the manner that meant something to *them,* they could always claim that while Wilkes had won a fight he had not conquered them and they were free to go on killing visitors as before.

The two young men took the message ashore and Wilkes prepared his men to land once again. They went to the appointed hill and waited.

So much had happened during the few days just past that Wilkes himself had not had time to digest it all. The deaths that had occurred had, momentarily at least, submerged the differences between Wilkes and his subordinate officers. The event had rendered Wilkes less harsh and less demanding for a while. He, of course, could not keep the thought of Midshipman Henry's mother from his mind. When the expedition returned to the United States, he would have to tell her the news and this thought both saddened and distracted him from his role as leader.

Waiting on the hilltop with his officers and men, Wilkes was affected by the scene, the events that had caused it and the memories that would linger.

"The day was perfectly serene," he wrote, "and the island, which, but a few hours before, had been one of the loveliest spots in creation, was now entirely laid waste, showing the place of the massacre, the ruined town, and the devastated plantations. The eye wandered over the dreary waste to the beautiful expanse of waters beyond and around, with the long lines of white sparkling reefs, until it rested, far in the distance, on the small green spot where we had performed the last rites to our murdered companions. A gentle breeze, which was blowing through the casuarina trees, gave out the moaning sound that is uttered by the pines of our own country, producing a feeling of depression inseparable from the occasion and bringing vividly to my thoughts the sad impression which this melancholy and dreadful occurrence would bring upon those who were far away."

The officers and men waited in the silence. Then, from far away across the island, came the sound of a native chant, a tuneless wail that grew louder and louder as the natives approached. They came to the foot of the hill on which Wilkes and his men stood waiting but would not come further until they had been assured that Wilkes would accept their surrender. Wilkes assured them of his intention to do just that.

True to his word, Wilkes put the old chief of Arro ashore when the surrender ceremonies had been completed. He also released the other prisoners. But by forcing the natives to surrender according to their own custom, Wilkes had definitely gained the upper hand. The islanders now considered the white men as their conquerors and they the expedition's slaves. To underscore his victory, Wilkes had several of the higher-ranking natives bring fresh water and food supplies to his ship. This the Fijis willingly did, for from that day onward the natives of Malolo considered that the white men owned the island which they had conquered.

It was the end of a chapter. The United States Exploring Expedition had completed its work in the Fiji Group. The surveying, the exploration by the naturalists, the soundings and magnetic and meteorological measurements all were stowed below decks and the ships once more prepared for sea. Early in August, the four-ship squadron stood out the narrow channel. The ships passed the coral reefs where the surf beat endlessly and then they were once more in the blue Pacific. The next rendezvous point: Honolulu, in what were then called the Sandwich Islands.

VOLCANIC CRATER ON MAUNA LOA

NO sooner had the four ships cleared the reef than they parted company. For Wilkes continued to take full advantage of the number of his ships to increase the range of his investigations. He ordered the *Porpoise* to nearby islands where Ringgold was to check the well-being of missionaries, warn native chieftains that missionaries and other visitors must not be molested, and also to survey the outlying reefs of that part of the seascape. When those chores were completed, Ringgold was to sail to the Samoan Islands once more and discover if the natives had yet captured the troublesome native chief, Opotuno. He was then to meet the other ships in Honolulu.

Wilkes ordered the *Flying Fish* to survey a long sea reef unconnected with any island but a hazard to mariners who could come upon it in fog or at night and be wrecked in an instant. When the small tender had finished the charting and the sounding needed to fix the position and extent of the reef exactly, she was to proceed to Honolulu.

On August 14, the *Vincennes* and *Peacock* parted company. Both were to sail on separate tracks for Honolulu. While en route, they were to search for islands that had been charted but rarely seen. These "doubtful islands" as Wilkes called them were spread over many charts of that day. For sailing ships, spotting a low-lying cloud on the horizon, could easily mistake it for land and plot it as such.

Thus occupied, the ships of the squadron made their individual ways toward the Sandwich Islands aiming for the rendezvous point of Honolulu on the large, central island of Oahu.

Today Hawaii is our fiftieth state and its inhabitants are citizens of the United States. During the time of Wilkes' voyage, the islands belonged to the Hawaiians as they had from prehistoric days. The various powers of the western world had taken note of the location and wealth of this particular group, and trading ships from European countries and the United States were found in the harbor in great numbers. The governments of the nationalities doing the trading with the Hawaiian people claimed that they were interested in preserving the sovereignty of the Hawaiian king and queen. They also claimed that their only interest was trading peacefully with the islanders and that for this reason they sometimes sent warships to the harbors of the island group just to be certain the natives were peaceful. Missionaries came to the islands and gradually the process of eroding the native culture was begun.

In days long before Wilkes, the English explorer James Cook had met an untimely death at the hands of the Sandwich Islanders. But that was during the late eighteenth century and now, as the mid-nineteenth century approached, a squadron of ships under such a commander as Wilkes could drop anchor in Honolulu and expect a cordial welcome not only by natives but by a large number of permanent white residents of the islands.

The *Vincennes* arrived off the harbor of Honolulu on September 24, 1840, and found the *Flying Fish* already there. The *Peacock* arrived on September 30 while the far-cruising *Porpoise* did not show up until October 8. But at last the squadron was together.

The arrival caused quite a stir. The *Vincennes,* for example, was greeted by what appeared to be nearly every inhabitant of the port city. They lined the beaches, the reefs, the walls, the fences, the balconies and the roofs of every building where sight of the ship could be obtained.

For a little while, it seemed to Wilkes that he was being accorded some of the honor that would come when he returned to the United States with the results of his voyages. The island of Oahu and the city of Honolulu were, judging by previous islands visited, civilized. Yet some of the problems of civilization became apparent to Wilkes shortly after his arrival. Since leaving the United

States, Wilkes had been free from harassment by senior officers in the Navy Department and free also from the indifference or self-seeking of politically minded Navy Department personnel. Arrival in Oahu changed that.

Through roundabout ways, news of Wilkes' claim to discovery of an Antarctic continent had reached Washington. And something else had reached Washington also: the English explorer James Clark Ross' claim that many of Wilkes' landfalls and positions of land given were false. Rumor had gotten around that Wilkes was mad. And one officer of the United States Navy—senior to Wilkes—stood up for Ross' claims of discovery of the Antarctic continent. He agreed with Ross, without having seen any of the evidence, that Wilkes' sightings and charted positions of Antarctic land indeed were false.

Another matter arose at Honolulu that spelled trouble for Wilkes when he returned to Washington at the end of the long voyage. Many of the expedition's men signed papers for a three-year enlistment and the time would be up on November 1, 1840. When that time came, some refused to reenlist and claimed that the government owed them transportation back to the United States. Wilkes saw the matter differently. He pointed to the terms of the papers they had signed which stipulated that the men would "return with the vessels to a port of safety in the United States." They could either reenlist and go on with the expedition until it returned, or make their own way home as best they could.

Several disgruntled men did just that—storing up

further trouble for Wilkes when he returned. As though to compound the problem, Wilkes hired on native islanders rather than white sailors to be found in the port of Honolulu. Wilkes' later claim was that the drunken flotsam available to him along the Honolulu waterfront would be of no use whatever in manning the ships in future months. The natives, on the other hand, were young and strong and clean. They did not drink and, further, they had the consent of their king and the governor of Oahu to enlist with the expedition. Wilkes was correct in his judgment that these men were better for him and, more to the point, that he had a legal right to hire "foreigners" if the conditions of employment were agreeable to all.

These matters took up much of Wilkes' thought during the first weeks of his stay in the Sandwich Island group. There were other matters to be decided also, however, and Wilkes turned to the problem of his expedition schedule and the time allowed to him to complete it.

According to the plan laid down long ago in Washington, the next area for exploration by the expedition squadron was to have been the Columbia River and the region then known as the Oregon Territory. But it was late in the year when Wilkes' last ship arrived safely in Oahu. Had he sent the squadron toward Oregon, they would not have arrived before the seasonal cold and rain had all but closed that area to exploration for the winter.

Wilkes decided to send his ships south to complete surveys and re-examine some faulty ones that had been made earlier. He also wanted Lieutenant Commandant Ringgold in the *Porpoise* to search for several natives who reportedly had killed white traders for no apparent reason.

While these cruises of the *Peacock, Porpoise* and *Flying Fish* were filling the winter months, Wilkes planned to ascend the famed volcanic peak of Mauna Loa on the island of Hawaii and make the same sort of survey he had completed in the Fiji Islands when he and his scientists had gone up the peak of Andulong. Following that, if time remained, he planned to take the *Vincennes* south and east of Honolulu to the Marquesas Islands and to sail easterly along the magnetic equator, plotting it as the *Porpoise* was to be doing to the west of the Sandwich Island group.

All ships were given orders to rendezvous next inside the bar of the famed Columbia River in Oregon Territory —a rendezvous easier to assign than to keep, as it turned out.

Early on the morning of December 3, 1840, the *Vincennes* left the harbor at Honolulu bound for the largest island of the group, Hawaii itself. The pilot who was supposed to guide the ship through the rather narrow channel to the sea failed to appear so Wilkes had the delicate job of taking his flagship out himself. To be on the safe side, he sent small boats to the edges of the channel and used them as marking buoys while the ship was maneuvered to deeper water. When the small craft and the boat crews had been safely taken aboard Wilkes set a course for Hawaii, the site of the famed volcanoes, Mauna Loa and Mauna Kea.

It was Wilkes' intention to take a large surveying party to the top of Mauna Loa where observations could be made and mapping accomplished that had never been done accurately before. In assigning himself to this task, Wilkes took on a job he liked and one where few of his fellow officers could have surpassed him.

Near Hilo, Wilkes established a sea level station where chronometers were checked, barometers compared and a schedule of simultaneous readings drawn up so that the party atop Mauna Loa and the shore-station party would take data together for comparison. Thus temperature, atmospheric pressure, magnetic readings and all other measurements would be made at the same time.

In planning his expedition, Wilkes studied the volcanic mountain carefully upon arriving at Hilo on the eastern side of the island. Unlike Mauna Kea—which was a typically cone-shaped volcano—Mauna Loa was more rounded in appearance and, as Wilkes noted, seemed not to be very high at all. It looked as though anyone could reach its summit in a few hours' walk. But Mauna Loa, like Andulong, proved deceptive.

To undertake this climb, Wilkes hired native bearers to carry supplies to the summit camps. Herds of animals for food were driven up the long, winding trail leading to the top.

Upon reaching it, Wilkes acknowledged the grandeur of the mountain which had appeared from a distance to be quite "tame."

"Just as we reached the great plain of the volcano, we approached the southern limit of the wood, and, on turning its corner, Mauna Loa burst upon us in all its grandeur. The day was extremely fine, the atmosphere pure and clean, except for a few flying clouds, and this immense dome rose before us from a plain some twenty miles in breadth. I had not, until then, formed any idea of its magnitude and height. The whole dome appeared of a bronze color, and its uninterrupted smooth outline was relieved against the deep blue of a tropical sky. . . . There was a bluish haze resting on the plain, that apparently gave it great distance, though this was partially counteracted by the distinctiveness of the dome. I now, for the first time, felt the magnitude of the task I had undertaken."

Not the least of Wilkes' chores was that of measuring the altitude of Mauna Loa and comparing it to the height of Mauna Kea in the distance. At that time, no one actually knew which of the two volcanoes was higher. From physical appearance, Mauna Kea seemed to be taller. But quick, rough measurements showed Mauna Loa to be very nearly as tall.

Upon reaching the summit, Wilkes found his party walking along the edge of the fantastic Mauna Loa crater over relatively insecure layers of lava. The crater itself at first did not impress Wilkes, for it appeared to be only a depression in the flat plain of the summit. On staring down into that gigantic cauldron, however, the expedition leader began to sense the majesty of this great changing mountain.

"What is wonderful in day," he wrote, "became ten times more so at night. The immense pool of cherry-red liquid lava, in a state of violent ebullition, illuminates the whole expanse, and flows in all directions like water, while the illuminated cloud hangs over it like a vast canopy."

Wilkes' journey up Mauna Loa and his establishment of an observation station was not as easy a task as it might seem today. The volcano, when Wilkes at last measured its height, proved to be 13,680 feet above sea level. Beyond the timber line nothing met his gaze but great masses and buttresses of lava. Snow capped the volcanic summit and it was bitterly cold. Native workers became discouraged and deserted. The men of the expedition suffered from what was then called "mountain sickness." This was nothing more than a deficiency of oxygen. Muscular weakness, shortness of breath, nausea upon the slightest exertion, nosebleeds and slight lung hemorrhages are symptoms of the lack of oxygen. During their entire stay on the summit, the men were hampered by the altitude.

Wilkes established a number of camps on the way to the top and he, himself, with observers and crewmen, set up instruments on the summit. The tents and supply caches were protected by walls of lava stone the men built around them. Each tent was thus protected and the encampment eventually had an additional wall built around it. Wilkes found this necessary since storms with hurricane-force winds frequently roared across the exposed peak. On several occasions, tents were blown down and instruments smashed by these gales.

As the days passed in this uncomfortable camp, the barometer, magnetometer, electroscopes, dip needles and thermometers were read at the agreed upon times to coincide with the readings at the sea-level camp in Hilo. Transits and the especially protected pendulum for measuring altitude were in use constantly as Wilkes worked to complete his survey. Occasional hikes to the crater and down below its rim brought lava samples for study and more temperature data for recording. Transits turned on neighboring Mauna Kea revealed that that volcano actually was a few feet higher than Mauna Loa. Wilkes determined the altitude of Mouna Kea as 13,784 feet while today's more careful measurements give 13,796 feet.

On January 13, 1841, Wilkes struck camp on the summit—the community known to the expedition as Pendulum Peak—and began to pack specimens, records and instruments for the return journey. The men who had suffered with Wilkes through the month-long exertion were so delighted to be leaving that they spontaneously gave three cheers when the last tent collapsed. Before departing, Wilkes instructed Jerome Clark to carve in the lava the words: Pendulum Peak, January

1841. Clark finished this task and then approached Wilkes, requesting that he also be permitted to carve the notation U. S. Ex.—Ex. so there would be no mistake about who had been there. Wilkes gladly consented to that addition and the men turned their steps down the volcano toward the ship.

With his work on the island of Hawaii completed, Wilkes decided to use the remaining winter weeks gathering data on the nearby island of Maui. The time of rendezvous with the *Porpoise* was approaching and Wilkes knew he would be unable to take the *Vincennes* to the Marquesas and return in time to make the agreed upon connection with his companion ship.

THE *Vincennes* and *Porpoise* sailed from Honolulu on April 5, 1841. Their destination: the famed and fearful bar across the mouth of the Columbia River. Twenty-three days after leaving the Sandwich Islands, the two ships stood off Cape Disappointment, the northern point of land marking the Columbia estuary.

Wilkes knew the difficulties of locating the channel through the treacherous sandbars guarding the river. Or at least he had read of them. But nothing in print could match the scene that met his eyes as the *Vincennes* approached the bar. From the mouth of the great river came flooding fresh water which met the inrushing water from the sea. The roar of surf was a constant, unending sound. The visible lines of surf on the hidden bars stretched across the entire mouth of the river from Cape Disappointment to Point Adams.

Wilkes had brought a man from the Sandwich Islands who claimed he could locate the channel and Wilkes was relying on him to get the ships through into the safe anchorage beyond the bar.

But for several days prior to the arrival of the *Vincennes* and *Porpoise,* gale winds and heavy seas had pounded the bar and the coast. The unbroken line of surf that met the gaze of the so-called pilot forced him to admit that he was useless. Wilkes dared not risk his ships until the weather moderated so he hauled off to deep water and lay to through the night.

Wilkes knew that British shipmasters and traders had marked a number of trees on Point Adams and Cape Disappointment by stripping them of branches except for a topmost bunch. These, if properly aligned and interpreted, would lead a ship to the channel. But neither Wilkes nor the alleged pilot knew the "combination" of the marked trees.

Nor would the British have willingly told Wilkes or any other United States vessel. For the region of the Oregon Territory was then in dispute. The British, through the Hudson's Bay Company, had established bases at various points in the territory and were claiming the land. The United States, on the other hand, was relatively weak in the area as far as official action was concerned. Citizens of the United States had penetrated to the shores of the Pacific and some settlement had been started, but Washington could not afford to back up whatever claims the settlers might want to put forward. It was, in effect, British territory and the officials of the Hudson's Bay Company were determined to keep it within the British Commonwealth. So the bar of the Columbia River was used by them as a powerful deterrent to exploration and colonization by sea on the part of the United States.

Wilkes realized the delicacy of his position. As an exploring expedition he had the right to expect hospitality and assistance from the friendly power of Britain. But he was also a United States naval officer and his ships were warships. As a naval officer, in fact, Wilkes had been given secret instructions to learn everything he could about the territory and give his opinion concerning the possible settlement of the region by United States citizens and a later claim to possession of the territory. So while Wilkes planned to go about the routine business of exploration, he also had a political-territorial question on his mind.

The gale winds and heavy seas off the river mouth did not slack off during the night. The *Vincennes*, at anchor in rough water, began shipping water through the hawse-holes, flooding the gun deck. Wilkes ordered the anchor chains unbent and the hawse-holes closed to keep the ship dry. He then made a decision to proceed northward to the Straits of Juan de Fuca and thence to Puget Sound where he also was ordered to go. The Columbia could wait. Wilkes took this decision in the interests of saving time. He had no way of knowing how long the bad weather would hold him off the bar. Nor did he know when the *Peacock* and *Flying Fish* would arrive. He, therefore, left word for the captain of the *Peacock* and made signal for the *Porpoise* to follow the *Vincennes* northward along the coast to the straits leading to Puget Sound.

Followed by the *Porpoise,* his flagship moved from small bay to bay, surveying harbors as she went. Wilkes sent an Indian to the nearest British post asking for a pilot to assist him in navigating the strange inshore waters of Puget Sound. When several days had passed, however, and the native had not returned, Wilkes cautiously continued his survey alone.

His personal reaction to Puget Sound was that it was a region of great beauty and, more to the point, of great utility. He found no dangerous shoals or other major hindrances to navigation. He realized that the many excellent harbors would take the world's largest vessels with ease, and that there was room for all the shipping in the world to anchor within the Sound, if need be.

Near the southern end of Puget Sound, off what then was called Fort Nisqually, the two ships dropped anchor. They were cordially welcomed by a Mr. Anderson, in charge of the British fort, and Captain McNeill, both of whom offered every courtesy to the explorers.

As soon as the ships had been safely moored and introductions between the Britishers and Wilkes' officers had been exchanged, Wilkes began planning his expedition's activities according to his instructions from Washington.

The *Porpoise,* with two of the small boats from the *Vincennes,* was to make a detailed survey and chart of Hood's Canal and Admiralty Inlet. A land party was organized under Lieutenant Johnson. He with several crewmen and a number of the scientific corps was to make an extensive journey. The lieutenant was ordered to take his party over the Cascade Range of mountains westward to the Columbia River, then south and as far west as Walla Walla. From there Johnson was ordered to return up the Yakima River, over the mountains again to rejoin the ships at Nisqually.

Wilkes himself was to lead another overland party, going south from Nisqually to Astoria and then to Fort Vancouver eastward along the Columbia as far as Walla Walla. Astoria, being near the mouth of the river, would be the ideal place to contact the *Peacock* and *Flying Fish.* Both vessels had been ordered to arrive by the time Wilkes traveled to the Hudson's Bay Company post at Astoria. Hoping to meet the other ships of the squadron there, Wilkes planned to have their small boats, under the officers of the *Peacock,* complete the survey of the lower Columbia River.

None of these inland expeditions was regarded lightly. They formed a major portion of the explorers' plans and goals. Eighty days, for example, were allotted to the party under Lieutenant Johnson, and during that time Wilkes hoped to cover the Columbia River from its mouth to Walla Walla. He also planned a side trip southward into the Willamette Valley.

Wilkes also had planned an extensive excursion when Captain Hudson arrived with the *Peacock* and *Flying Fish*. In addition to needing the boats from these ships for river surveying and charting, he wanted Hudson to go eastward up the Columbia and across the Rocky Mountains on an exploratory mission. There were, in short, few places of importance in the Oregon Territory to which Wilkes did not send a party.

In all places that he and his officers visited, Wilkes found American settlers living harmoniously with British subjects employed by the famous Hudson's Bay Company. Wilkes also noticed the fertility of many parts of the country. In the Willamette Valley, for example, he talked with settlers who admitted that the introduction of whiskey would be the ruination of them. They had, therefore, all agreed to be abstemious. The reason was not primarily the whiskey, but the small amount of time necessary for them to work to produce a living. Wilkes was assured that one month's work a year would make a man a living. This undemanding life, the settlers felt, could prove fatal if whiskey were introduced, for its temptation would be difficult to resist with all the leisure time at their disposal. Wilkes found wheat growing seven feet tall on the banks of the Columbia River. Corn grew to nine feet and all vegetables and grains were produced in plenty with minimum cultivation. Over all the area, Wilkes saw cattle increasing, growing fat on the limitless grazing grass available.

By horseback and by boat, Wilkes and his various parties explored the territory that later was to become the states of Washington and Oregon. The naturalists gathered specimens of plant and animal life they had never seen before. Geologists collected rock specimens and the interminable mapping and surveying continued. On returning to Nisqually from one of his journeys, Wilkes learned that the huts he had ordered built to house the pendulum equipment were complete and these experiments were immediately undertaken. Magnetic and electroscopic readings were also recorded periodically.

The days were hurrying by and Wilkes had not heard from the *Peacock* and the *Flying Fish*. He had earlier received a report that they had arrived safely at the mouth of the Columbia River but this proved to be false. His original orders stated that the *Peacock* was to be at the Columbia River not later than May first. But May had passed—and June and most of July—with no sign of the missing vessels. Wilkes himself, at Nisqually, was completing his extensive survey of large portions of Puget Sound. And as the days passed, he grew more and more apprehensive regarding the missing ships. The uneasiness spread among officers and the men. If the ships were lost, much of the further work of the expedition would fall on men already having full schedules.

On July 20, Wilkes aboard the *Vincennes* ordered the

flagship to New Dungeness near the entrance of that long narrow passage within Puget Sound called Hood's Canal. Here the *Porpoise* joined the flagship and the two ships sailed shortly through the Straits of de Fuca and turned south along the coast toward the rendezvous at the mouth of the Columbia.

The *Peacock* and *Flying Fish* indeed were late. On sailing south from Oahu months before, the two-ship squadron under the command of Captain Hudson began another cruise among the South Sea Islands in accordance with Wilkes' orders. They were to check some of the earlier surveys, search for islands charted once by earlier explorers but never located again, and also search for several white men who apparently had gone native, abandoning ships and families for the life of ease on the white sand beaches of the Pacific. They also were to try once again to capture the elusive Samoan chief Opotuno.

Captain Hudson undertook his mission seriously and he carried out all surveys and searches in great detail—in fact so accurate were his charts of the areas in which he sailed that over a hundred years later the U. S. Navy found itself using them during World War II. But Hudson forgot the time. He let day follow day while his enthusiasm for his work kept everyone concentrated on the task at hand.

In this delay he was seriously endangering the expedition's ability to carry out the remainder of its program, and there was much left to be done in even more distant seas.

But when Captain Hudson had completed all his assignments (save capturing Opotuno, who permanently eluded capture) he set a course for the Columbia River arriving off Cape Disappointment July 17. He had with him the best available instructions for navigating the channel into the river mouth, instructions which had come from British sources and supposedly were easily followed.

At least as Captain Hudson maneuvered the *Peacock* toward the surfline on the bar he believed there would be no great problem taking his ship through the channel to a safe anchorage within the broad mouth of the river.

The morning of July 18 dawned foggy with poor visibility. It was a Sunday. Captain Hudson proceeded cautiously along the coast waiting for the fog to clear which it did around eight o'clock. Cape Disappointment was plainly visible about nine miles away. A sounding taken at nine that morning revealed a bottom at forty fathoms. An hour later it was only fifteen fathoms.

In the morning light, the line of breakers over the treacherous bar was visible. The *Peacock* tacked offshore while Hudson completed his preparations to cross the bar.

He sent Lieutenant Emmons aloft to the foretopsail yard while he himself, holding the precisely written instructions for finding the channel in his hand, took charge of the ship. At this time the *Peacock* was running northeast, a quarter east, heading for Cape Disappointment. He held that course until bringing Chinook Point onto an east-northeast heading. Instead of a channel ahead, all Hudson or Emmons could see were breakers. Captain Hudson changed course abruptly and headed away from shore for another try.

Lieutenant Perry joined Lieutenant Emmons in the rigging to help spot the channel. Hudson turned the *Peacock* toward shore once more and this time, from the deck and from the rigging, there appeared a break in the line of surf marking the bar.

The helmsman steered for it. It appeared smooth and its position agreed with the sailing directions Hudson had in his hand. Within minutes the *Peacock* was aground.

The instant Hudson felt the keel strike he ordered "Hard alee." The helmsman spun the wheel and every attempt was made to bring the ship off. But almost immediately the *Peacock* began to pound.

Lieutenant Emmons scrambled down from aloft and went overside in a small boat to assess the situation of the ship. By this time the *Peacock* had become completely unmanageable and Captain Hudson ordered sail furled. A kedging anchor and cable went overside into Lieutenant Emmons' boat. With it, Hudson hoped to pull the *Peacock* from the sandbar. But each rise and fall of the sea drove the ship farther on the bar. The wind shifted to northwest and the ebb tide from the river mouth met incoming waves and the onshore wind. Waves broke all around the stranded *Peacock*. Even the small boats with the kedging gear were threatened. A wave threw one boat against the hull of the ship, crushing her planking. Lieutenant Emmons brought his boat in the lee of the ship. All hope of setting the kedging anchor in deep water and pulling the *Peacock* off had to be abandoned. The waves tossed the small boat so violently the crew had all they could do to stay afloat. When it became evident that the men could not survive long in that sea, Hudson ordered a line thrown down to the men and the boat finally was secured.

The *Peacock* herself was leaking badly and Hudson ordered pumps started. Everyone aboard knew from the sound of the ship's keel striking the sandbar that she was doomed.

As the waves rose and the destruction of the ship approached, Hudson and his men went on trying to save her. Hudson believed that if he could get the ship's bow turned into the waves, she would last longer and might be floated off on the next high tide—if the storm subsided and the hull remained intact.

As the ship rose on the oncoming waves, the men struggled with the helm to take advantage of the few seconds she was off the bar and tried to turn her around. But after a few attempts, they were stopped completely. The metal tiller snapped and the rudder slammed back and forth uncontrollably, at the mercy of the sea.

Hudson ordered all available men to lighten the ship by throwing supplies, ballast and the supply of cannonballs overboard. The larboard anchor had been let go and was hooked into the bottom some distance from the ship. As darkness approached, the men hauled in on the anchor chain, turning the bow at last to the oncoming sea.

Hudson breathed a sigh of relief for it appeared, momentarily at least, that he might have a chance to save his ship. The tide continued to ebb and the *Peacock* tossed fitfully on the sandbar waiting for the turn of the tide and the subsidence of the angry sea.

Then without warning the anchor chain snapped and the *Peacock* turned broadside to the oncoming waves. As the tide turned and came flooding toward high water, the storm increased in the darkness sending waves completely over the foundering ship. The waves crushed bulwarks and flooded the spardeck. Water rose in the ship, filling the shot lockers and reaching knee height on the gundeck.

Hudson wondered whether his ship would stay together throughout the night. He had all pumps manned but the pounding sea opened more planking with each passing minute—and more water poured in.

At dawn, again a low tide, the storm finally subsided and a canoe from the shore manned by Indians approached the wrecked ship. Aboard the native boat were a pilot and a crew member of the *Vincennes* who had been left at Astoria to wait for the ships.

Hudson saw that the sea had calmed enough to put over his boats and he ordered them hoisted out and loaded with records and provisions. Under the command of Lieutenant Emmons, they made their way toward shore.

The boats reached Baker's Bay successfully. The sick men from the ship, the naturalists with their papers and specimens, and all but those needed to work the boats, were put ashore. The boats returned to the *Peacock* where they found her filling with water, lower on the sandbar and with the remaining men busy cutting away masts and rigging.

With the completion of the second trip to shore, only about thirty-five officers and men remained aboard ship. Lieutenant Emmons started the boats from shore on a third journey but by this time the sea had risen again and the waves threatened his boats. Nevertheless, Emmons ordered boat captains to try to reach Hudson and their remaining shipmates.

The waves rose rapidly over the bar and one boat under the command of a gunner named Lewis rose on a curling breaker and turned completely over, end over end. All the men were thrown into the water. Lieutenant De Haven's boat picked up the wet and injured men and returned to shore. The others continued to try to reach the ship. But Hudson on the *Peacock* had seen the accident and he hoisted a flag signaling the boat commanders to turn back and wait for calmer weather.

Lieutenant Emmons took his boats to shore. He was as aware as Captain Hudson that if the boats were lost, the men aboard the ship were lost, too. During all these hours, while water gradually rose in the ship and the waves crashed against her hull, Captain Hudson maintained complete shipboard routine. He had watches piped, dinner served at the usual hour and all the chores attended to. At 3:00 P.M. Lieutenant Emmons tried once more to get his boats out to the ship but again he was driven back.

Two hours later he set out again. The wind had

slacked off and during the lull he managed to take off all the remaining men and officers. As soon as they had been rescued, the boats made for Baker's Bay where Hudson's arrival was greeted with cheers from the men waiting on shore.

Everyone had been saved. And although supplies and some of the expedition material had been lost, most had been taken safely ashore. Yet Hudson wanted to have one more try at salvaging material and the next morning he set out with the boats toward the derelict *Peacock*. But when they reached the bar, the ship was gone—all except the cap of her bowsprit. Planks, ribs, masts, yards, rigging, decks and all supplies and remaining records scattered overnight along the inhospitable shore.

When Wilkes heard of the loss of the *Peacock* he immediately began planning his adjustment to that unhappy event. His official report of Hudson's handling of the ship saved that officer from court-martial but Wilkes could not help feeling that Hudson was more than a little to blame. In the first place, Wilkes reasoned, the *Flying Fish* of lighter draft should have been the first vessel to approach the dangerous bar. In the second, he felt Hudson and his officers should have steered not for the dead smooth water they mistook for the channel but rather for the opening in the line of breakers where tide ripples showed the quantity of water surging through the true channel.

There had been no question of Hudson's seamanship save for the impetuous way he had approached the hazardous mouth of the river. His actions, as Wilkes was quick to point out, after the *Peacock* had gone aground were the subject for praise, not blame of any kind.

Wilkes' harshest judgment of Hudson was not centered on the wreck of the *Peacock*. It was the nearly three-month delay in arriving at the rendezvous. This seriously upset the expedition's timetable and in the light of that lost time as well as the lost ship, Wilkes had to make radical adjustments.

He transferred himself from the *Vincennes* to the *Porpoise* and placed Lieutenant Commandant Ringgold in command of his former flagship. The *Vincennes* he ordered to San Francisco to undertake a survey of the Sacramento River and part of San Francisco Bay. During the time the *Vincennes* was in California, Wilkes planned to undertake the extensive survey of the Columbia River to the "extreme of its navigability."

The *Vincennes* sailed for San Francisco and Wilkes, left with the smaller *Porpoise*, realized that the efficiency of the expedition was suffering from the loss of the one ship. With characteristic vigor, he decided to do something about it. At anchor in the Columbia River at that time lay an American brig, the *Thomas H. Perkins*, a trading vessel. Wilkes offered to purchase the ship and the matter was speedily settled. Under the command of one of his officers, Wilkes ordered his new ship—which he renamed the *Oregon*—into Vancouver for alteration.

Following that task she was to sail to San Francisco and join the *Vincennes* there.

During the long months Wilkes and his men were in the Oregon Territory, no one, least of all any of the Hudson's Bay Company officials, was fooled about one of the aims of the exploring expedition. That they were there to "spy out" the territory was obvious. And Wilkes accomplished this in an admirable fashion. He mapped the territory as no one else had ever done and with such thoroughness that his survey and subsequent report of the potential of that area had much to do with its settlement by United States citizens. Wilkes recognized that the Oregon Territory could be more easily reached by citizens of the United States than by British subjects coming down from Canada. He also noted—and reported—the number of white settlers in the region carefully distinguishing between the number of Canadians present and the number of United States citizens.

One of Wilkes' most ambitious projects, that of sending a party east of the Rocky Mountains to scout a way for settlers to enter the territory, had to be abandoned. Before leaving Oregon, however, Wilkes did send out an overland party which left Fort Vancouver and trekked southward toward California under the command of Lieutenant Emmons.

As usual, Wilkes' instructions to the lieutenant spelled out everything the commander expected of his subordinate.

Emmons was to proceed from Fort Vancouver through

the Willamette Valley passing to the west of Mount Shasta to the headwaters of the Sacramento River which he then was to follow, as nearly as possible, to San Francisco.

Along the way, Wilkes' orders read, he was to avoid any "collision" with Indians but was not to appear to be avoiding them. When he had passed through the hostile Indian territory, Emmons was given the alternative of proceeding by horseback or building canoes and proceeding down the Sacramento River waterway.

All along the route, Wilkes ordered observations and surveys carried on as extensively as possible. In his instructions, he passed on as many hints as he could to assist the overland party. He explained how distances to remote objects could be determined by laying off a long baseline—using the pace of a horse as a measuring unit—for the triangulation problem. He also ordered Emmons to "Attend to the velocity of rivers by the distance that a chip will pass in any given number of seconds by your watch . . ."

All along the way, Emmons was to take barometric and temperature readings every six hours. And Wilkes remembered to remind the lieutenant that "If by any accident your barometer should be broken on the heights, try the temperature at which water boils."

In one instruction, Wilkes asked for information that could have taken a party twice as large a year or more to complete. "The information also expected from your party will be names of tribes, numbers, manners, customs, mode of living, habits, character disposition and incidents that may occur to the party, as also the timber, kinds and quality, soils, climate, etc. And if you meet with any settlers note their condition, whence from, etc."

Little wonder that the officers under Wilkes complained about his excessive detail in issuing orders! Several had already complained that Wilkes was so meticulous he could not send an officer forward of the quarterdeck without issuing "sailing directions."

But with his expedition split into numerous parties most of the time, Wilkes had good reason to issue detailed orders. It was the only way he could be certain his program would be accomplished and all the ships and shore parties would come together again—as they finally did in San Francisco Bay.

Lieutenant Commandant Ringgold with the *Vincennes* had preceded Wilkes down the coast. The *Oregon* left Vancouver, her alterations completed, and went directly to San Francisco and then Wilkes himself aboard the *Porpoise* arrived in the harbor. And, last but not least, Lieutenant Emmons and his party arrived after traveling through the rugged country north of San Francisco.

Their path had been beset with some danger, since from the Willamette Valley to what were called the Boundary Mountains on the northern border of California, hostile Indians had been reported at the last Hudson's Bay fort in the upper Willamette region. Word in fact had come to the Hudson's Bay men at that fort that the Indians were massing to halt the white men's passage. Lieutenant Emmons took all reasonable precautions and proceeded on his way. Throughout their journey they kept strict guard over the camp and the few Indians they saw were waved away when they attempted to approach. On their journey, Emmons and his men came across several grim reminders of Indian savagery. In one spot, the site of a famous massacre of several years before, the explorers found skeletons and skulls of victims of the attack. The sight kept them alert for the remainder of their journey through the hostile country. In one way this was an unfortunate state of affairs, for one of the principal purposes of the journey was to study the Indians and bring back information as Wilkes had instructed. But close-range examination of the natives of that region was denied the lieutenant.

Wild game throughout their journey was plentiful. Deer, elk—as large as horses—and grizzly bears plus wolves made for lively hunting at all times. On one occasion as the party journeyed along its final leg of exploration down the Sacramento River, Emmons decided to ford the river at one point on the opposite bank of which was a place named Bear Camp. The party's Indian hunter had preceded the group and was found already in camp—with the skin and meat of a fresh-killed grizzly beside him. Emmons and his men passed over the river at the fording place and that afternoon men of the party shot five more grizzly bears all within sight of camp.

With all his ships and all his men back together once more, Wilkes prepared for the next phase of his journey. He had already had to curtail the program because of Hudson's delay in reaching the Columbia River from the South Pacific. This meant that his instructions regarding exploration along the coast of Japan and in the seas of the Orient could be carried out only in a limited way.

But first, he had to rid himself of the horses and saddles and other equipment of the shore party. An auction was held before the squadron departed and the worn horses and saddles were quickly bought up by the Californians who formed the communities around San Francisco Bay.

November 1, 1841, found the four-ship squadron putting out from San Francisco and very nearly found the *Vincennes* being wrecked on the San Francisco bar as the *Peacock* had been lost.

As the ships stood down San Francisco Bay, they found the winds light and contrary with the tide against them. Shortly after sunset, the wind died altogether. Aboard the *Vincennes* once more, Wilkes signaled the other ships to heave to for the night. They were several miles to seaward of the flagship and dropped anchor in relatively deep water. The *Vincennes* was just inside a bar in about seven fathoms (42 ft.) of water. Wilkes ordered sail furled and the anchor let go. Unknown to him, his ship was in the most dangerous position he could have chosen. For a peculiar effect of the tide flooding over the bar out beyond the *Vincennes* was to set up a tremendous set of waves for the time of the tide's coming. This periodic disturbance was confined to the sandbar itself and the water directly behind it—exactly where the *Vincennes* lay anchored.

When the sun set that night, Wilkes noted the calm water, the placid weather and went to his cabin for a good night's rest. About 10:00 P.M. a long swell ran under the ship's keel, and then another and another. Wilkes awoke with a feeling of anxiety and went on deck. The tide had begun to come to flood. The ship was engulfed not only in the blackness of the night but also in a dense fog. Yet the roar of breakers and the violent pitching of the ship told her commander that they were in trouble.

By midnight this strange situation had become even more critical. The *Vincennes* rode at the end of her anchor chain like a dog pulling on a leash as the waves increased in height. Wilkes ordered more chain paid out to get as far from the bar as possible and to give the ship greater ability to ride with the increasingly high waves. By 3:00 A.M. the waves were thirty feet high breaking over the ship's bow, flooding the decks and sweeping everything before them. Occasionally the ship turned broadside to the onrushing breakers and then rolled, as Wilkes put it, "so deep as to endanger our masts."

Accustomed as he was to high seas and storms, Wilkes was alarmed by these great waves which he could not escape. For if he let go his anchor chain the ship would turn broadside to the surf, helpless in its grip. Since there was no wind, there was little use in raising sail. All Wilkes could do was hang on.

"At 2:00 A.M.," Wilkes reported, "a breaker was

heard outside of us, passing in with the roar of a surf, after which they became constant and really awful. The ship might now be said to be riding in breakers of gigantic size; they rushed onwards with such a tremendous roar and violence that, as each wave was heard approaching, it became a source of apprehension until it had safely passed.

"Such was its force that when it struck the ship, the chain cable would surge, the ring-stoppers part, and some few fathoms of cable escape. As the time of high water approached, the roar of these immense breakers was constant. The ship was as if tempest-tossed, and our situation became at each moment one of greater solicitude."

Despite the critical situation, Wilkes reasoned that if the anchor chain parted, the tide would sweep the *Vincennes* into deep water within the harbor where they would be safe. But there was always the problem of being struck broadside and severely damaged if not sunk before the ship reached the safety of the deep harbor.

Such a condition very nearly did occur. At 3:00 A.M. a breaker struck the ship "broad on the bow." The cable surged and the ring stoppers were carried away. The spar-deck was swept fore and aft. Boats and booms broke free. The boats were crushed and the booms crashed against the rail. A crewman, struck by a loose spar, was killed almost instantly.

But he was the only casualty of that restless night. By eight o'clock the next morning the waves were no longer breaking over the ship. A light breeze sprang up and Wilkes ordered sail set and the anchor weighed. The *Vincennes* moved out toward the sea to join the other ships.

The squadron set a course for the Sandwich Islands once more. Wilkes had not intended to return there but the loss of the *Peacock* and nearly all of the men's equipment and clothing made it necessary to replenish supplies somewhere—and Honolulu was the nearest "civilized" port since the sleepy little town of San Francisco at that time was no more than an assemblage of ranches on the shores of the bay.

The four-ship squadron arrived in the harbor at Honolulu on November 17, 1841. There the officers and men were received in as friendly a fashion as before. But Wilkes was in a hurry. A look ahead at the remainder of his schedule gave him good reason for haste.

His instructions called for extensive exploration of the Japanese coast and the Japanese islands. But he also was ordered to make a survey of coastal lands in the East Indies and Southeast Asia—as we know it today. He was then to sail with his squadron around the Cape of Good Hope and return to the United States across the Atlantic, completing his four-year voyage.

Ten days after reaching Honolulu, Wilkes ordered the ships to sail on the next phase of the squadron's work. And although time was short, he did not eliminate Japan from his program. Shortly after clearing Honolulu harbor, Wilkes signaled his ships to heave to while he completed orders for them. Once more the squadron was to split.

Wilkes sent the *Porpoise* and *Oregon*—under the senior commander Ringgold of the *Porpoise*—on a west and northwest cruise along the whaling grounds of the Pacific to search for and chart possible hazards to ships. "There are," as Wilkes wrote to Ringgold, "many dangerous shoals and reefs said to exist, and of which we have little accurate knowledge."

Thus the two ships were to travel westward, fanning out during daylight hours to cover as large an area as possible "keeping two good men at the lookout," as Wilkes admonished.

When Ringgold approached the coast of Japan he was to search for the current said to exist (now known as the Japanese Current) along its shores. He then was to take the two ships into the China Sea by the Formosa Passage and proceed to Singapore where he would rejoin the *Vincennes* and the *Flying Fish*.

Wilkes, meantime, planned to cruise in search of many islands and shoals marked doubtful on the charts. His course lay west of the Sandwich Island group and, on one foray northward, the *Vincennes* dropped anchor off Wake Island (then called Wake's Island) where naturalists went ashore and specimens of plant and animal life were gathered.

Day after day, cruising south and west, the *Vincennes* passed over positions showing islands and found nothing but the restless blue-green Pacific Ocean. The *Flying Fish* had parted company with the *Vincennes*. Shortly after leaving Honolulu, the captain of the tender reported that he thought the tender's mainmast had been sprung. Inspection by a carpenter sent over from the *Vincennes* revealed nothing, but Wilkes, rather than be delayed by the possibly defective vessel, ordered her captain to proceed on his own.

On January 10, 1842, the *Vincennes* was in sight of Manila Bay, but light winds—or no wind at all—kept the flagship from entering the harbor. As the *Vincennes* was trying to reach an anchorage, the *Flying Fish* appeared and together the two vessels finally managed to reach their goal.

In Wilkes' day the Philippine Islands belonged to Spain, and Manila was an important port as well as a harbor where ships of all nations came for supplies, refitting and trade. So Wilkes' principal work here was simply the meeting of the governor, paying a courtesy visit before proceeding into more dangerous waters.

Sailing south from Manila, the *Vincennes* and *Flying Fish* surveyed the coastal shores and sounded the waters off the southern end of the Island of Mindoro. The two ships then entered the Sooloo Sea (now spelled Sulu) where pirates from the principal island of Sooloo frequently raided shipping and caused trouble for United States vessels. The Sooloo natives under a sultan were Mohammedans and still very active in the capturing of slaves.

Wilkes headed for the village where the Sooloo sultan lived. In his report of the several days the two ships spent there, Wilkes makes it plain that he regarded the Sooloos as vicious, treacherous, dirty and cowardly.

Yet his instructions had been to conclude a treaty, if at all possible, with the sultan in an attempt to make the future presence of United States vessels a safer experience than it had been in the past.

Wilkes' feeling about these particular natives was well expressed in one account of the theft by a Sooloo native of the pistol belonging to one of the *Vincennes'* officers.

Wilkes told the local official known as a datu that he wanted the pistol returned and that there would be trouble if no action were taken. A day and a night passed with no response coming from the datu. So the evening of the second day, Wilkes took the steps he thought necessary to bring the pistol back aboard ship. Ordinarily at sunset, it was the ship's custom to fire an evening gun—a small brass cannon of no size at all. But Wilkes had noticed how the sound echoed and re-echoed about the harbor in which the *Vincennes* was anchored. He decided to load the largest gun on the ship and touch it off. When he did, the entire island seemed to shake and the sound reverberated as never before across the village rooftops. Watching the shore, Wilkes saw several of the Sooloo natives run out of their huts and stare at the ship. Some gathered on the shore in a state of excitement and then left, still talking and glancing back over their shoulders.

Wilkes slept comfortably that night, certain that the warning sound had been enough. And sure enough, the next morning a boat put out from shore, the datu came aboard with the missing pistol and said that he had spent the entire night searching for it. Everyone apologized and, outwardly at least, friendly relations had been restored.

Before leaving the Sooloo Sea, Wilkes did sign a treaty of friendship with the sultan which was his principal aim in going to the area in the first place. In effect, the treaty granted the United States favorable trading terms under the full protection of the sultan; a promise of assistance in case any United States vessel foundered or was wrecked in the waters within the sultan's "Domain;" a further promise that if any of the sultan's subjects caused "injury or harm" to officers or crews of American vessels, they would be punished by the sultan to the extent of their crimes.

Just how conscientious the sultan or his successors might be in carrying out the terms of that treaty was a matter of some doubt in Wilkes' mind at the time of signing. But the forceful part of the situation was that if the United States learned of a case where the sultan had failed to live up to the terms, the United States could then take whatever action it felt necessary.

Wilkes had detached the *Flying Fish* once more and sent it on a further survey of reefs and islands in the immediate area of the Sooloo Sea. He had instructed her commander, Knox, to rendezvous at Singapore. On February 18, 1842, the *Vincennes* herself dropped anchor in the Strait of Singapore and the next day sailed into the harbor.

Singapore was the last rendezvous for the squadron. The orders, written years before, had stated that the expedition was to return by May 31, 1842, and accordingly Wilkes laid his plans for the long voyage home to the United States.

After much consultation with his officers and experts in the port of Singapore he decided that the expense of refitting the *Flying Fish* and nursing that small vessel across thousands of miles of ocean would be more expensive than disposing of the vessel in the Far Eastern port. He reached this conclusion reluctantly, however, since as he reported ". . . I still felt a strong inclination to persist in bringing her back to the United States. . . . To part with the vessel was unpleasant on many accounts; for she had been daily, for nearly four years, my first and last thought. The attachment I had felt for her was great; the efficient aid she had occasionally afforded in the performance of my duties, caused me to value her highly; and as a sea vessel of her class she was almost faultless."

Nonetheless, the *Flying Fish* was put up for public auction and sold for $3700.

Wilkes wrote orders for the *Porpoise* and *Oregon,* sending them through the Indian Ocean, around Cape of Good Hope, to the island of St. Helena and across the south Atlantic to Rio de Janiero. From that South American port visited so long ago, the ships were to sail for New York. Upon arrival there, Lieutenant Commandant Ringgold was instructed to give each man ten dollars and release him immediately, since in very nearly all instances the terms of enlistment would have expired. Ringgold was to retain a crew of volunteers as shipkeepers until other Navy personnel took over the two brigs.

The *Vincennes* was to take a slightly different route but all ships continued their observations of tides, currents, sea and air temperatures, air-pressure readings, magnetic readings and all the other data-taking that had marked the extended voyage around the world.

Wilkes aboard the *Vincennes* arrived in New York Harbor on June 15, 1842, and a pilot came on board. A steamer took the ship in tow. There was a brief stop at quarantine for a visit by the health officer and then the *Vincennes* moved slowly up the bay toward the Battery and the end of the long voyage.

"Before I left the *Vincennes,*" Wilkes reported, "the crew were called to muster, when I expressed to them my thanks for the manner in which they had conducted themselves during the cruise, and stated the confident belief entertained by me, that they would receive from the government such rewards as the successful performance of the cruise and their long and perilous services, entitled them to. A national salute was then fired, and my pennant hauled down. . . . As soon as she (the *Vincennes*) was safely moored, all the men who could be spared were allowed to go on shore, with their bags and hammocks. A happier set of fellows than they were is not often met with; being relieved from their long confinement on shipboard, and the severe discipline of a man-of-war."

No bands or cheering crowds greeted the returning explorers. There was only a curious silence that was more than the quiet of indifference. To Wilkes it seemed ominous.

CHARLES WILKES U.S.N.

INCREDIBLE events followed within days of Wilkes' return to the United States. He and his officers and men had been gone four years. They had completed the most extensive exploration of the planet that the young United States had ever undertaken—as extensive an expedition as any country in the world before or since has undertaken.

Here, in brief summary, is what Wilkes accomplished:

The expedition had circumnavigated the globe increasing the number of soundings to the benefit of all shipping everywhere.

The South Polar regions had been defined as a continent and future claims of the United States in Antarctica would be based on Wilkes' sightings.

Two hundred and eighty separate islands had been surveyed and a total of 180 charts constructed for the benefit of mariners and geographers the world around.

An important survey of the Oregon Territory had been accomplished and the area had been mapped. In his reports Wilkes pointed out routes that settlers could follow, likely points for military installations, and ways of coping with both the country and its inhabitants in the future years of western expansion to the Pacific.

Specimens in all branches of botanical and zoological studies were brought back in profusion. The scientific gains for the young United States fulfilled the dreams of former President John Quincy Adams and provided the basis for a national natural history museum.

The expedition itself had been successfully managed and with few exceptions all the orders given Wilkes had been fulfilled.

Yet when the ships returned, no one met them. The officers and men went ashore amid the stares of a few curious bystanders. The expedition members scattered to their homes. Wilkes himself rejoined his wife and children, and waited for some recognition that the United States Exploring Expedition had completed its objective.

None came.

Wilkes decided to pay a call on the President.

During his absence there had been a change of administration. Martin Van Buren had been defeated and John Tyler now headed the administration. Of importance to Wilkes was the fact that Tyler and his cabinet were busily creating the impression that everything Van Buren had done was wrong—which included sending out the United States Exploring Expedition.

So Wilkes went to the White House where he found Tyler, according to one report, sitting before a fire with a number of his friends spitting tobacco juice on the blazing logs. Tyler greeted Wilkes by shaking his hand and asking if he would like to sit down and join the group. Wilkes did sit down but during his short time with the President and his friends, no one so much as mentioned the exploring expedition. Wilkes finally left.

Next he called on the Secretary of the Navy, who neither shook his hand nor asked him if he would like to sit down. The Navy Department along with many high-ranking naval officers had already begun to disown Wilkes.

Mr. Upshur, the Secretary of the Navy, listened coldly to Wilkes' request for at least some civilized recognition of the return of the expedition, but all Mr. Upshur did was to inform Wilkes that he expected all reports, records and specimens and reports of the expedition be turned over to him at Wilkes' earliest convenience.

Wilkes returned to his home deeply concerned. It was

evident that he was going to be shoved into oblivion just as fast as possible by politicians and service personnel who, for one reason or another, held a grudge against him.

Wilkes turned to the Congress where he had important friends and on the advice of one of them, organized a lecture to discuss the results of the expedition. It was the only way he could think to bring the expedition to the attention of the nation.

The objects of natural history and the artifacts from the primitive people of the Pacific had been gathered together and put on display in the Patent Office. The lecture was held in a large hall of that building and Wilkes outlined the results of the four-year voyage. He had a distinguished audience composed of senators and representatives plus cabinet officials—including Navy Secretary Upshur.

Wilkes raised the question as to why the expedition was being ignored by official Washington and then proceeded to explain why by calling the names of people present. When he sat down, a round of applause encouraged him to think that he had persuaded his audience that an injustice was being done, not only to him but also to the officers and men who had served faithfully and well for four long years.

To his surprise, Secretary Upshur rose and complimented Wilkes, praising what a day or so before he had ignored. The Secretary further suggested that the entire assemblage vote Wilkes their appreciation for his accomplishment. It was apparently a satisfactory meeting.

Wilkes went home feeling he and his men might get the credit they deserved.

What Wilkes got was a court-martial.

Shortly after the lecture at the Patent Office, the commander of the United States Exploring Expedition was informed that charges were being preferred against him by the Secretary of the Navy himself, Mr. Upshur.

Two men in particular who had served on the expedition supplied the Secretary of the Navy with reports on which the charges were based. One of the men was assistant surgeon Guillou and the other was Lieutenant Pinkney. Eleven charges and over thirty specifications were brought against Wilkes in September, approximately three months after his return.

Among the items of complaint were cruelty, scandalous conduct, oppression, illegal punishment and various alleged violations of the law. Back of most of them lay the personal and private grudges of the complainants. The administration at that time also demonstrated its eagerness to bring Wilkes down by having brought the charges and specifications together so hastily that in the end he either was found not guilty or the charge was dropped with but one exception: The extra lashes he had ordered given to the crew members on one occasion were regarded as excessive by the officers of the court, and as a result, Wilkes was given a public reprimand.

In one charge, Wilkes was accused of falsifying his records of sighting Antarctic land. And while this charge was proven untrue and dropped, it gave rival nations interested in discrediting Wilkes a firm toehold. If his own government, they could say, charged the explorer with falsification of land sightings and if their own explorers could show that some of Wilkes' positions for land were false, then they could discredit him completely.

In looking at all the effort to send Wilkes into a kind of historical oblivion, it is necessary to ask what prompted it. Basically there were three reasons:

1. Wilkes' own personality which lacked warmth and which had what we today would call snobbishness in large measure. He was no handshaking, smiling, hero type. He made enemies easily and on the voyage of four years his concern over the degree of personal success and national success that would result from his efforts frequently made him more of a martinet than the occasion demanded.

2. The political maneuvering both in the Navy and in the Administration. A man absent for four years, having personnel returning with grudges, can come back to find himself already condemned for real or fancied causes.

3. The eagerness of foreign governments to claim new lands in the Antarctic and to discredit the claims of young, upstart countries as the United States was then.

The exploring expedition of which Wilkes was the commander was the first such venture the United States had put out. It was watched with considerable apprehension by other governments—particularly England—and while courtesies were maintained, no one doubted that this major challenge by the United States was serious.

One of Wilkes' most implacable enemies turned out to be an Englishman that Wilkes hoped would be a helpful friend: James Clark Ross. When Wilkes returned to Sydney from his major second venture into the Antarctic he wrote a lengthy letter to Ross who was to arrive in Sydney in his two ships the *Erebus* and *Terror* after Wilkes had left those latitudes. In this letter Wilkes offered what assistance he could, telling the rival what land he had sighted and what the results of the voyage had been. It was a generous gesture for which Wilkes paid dearly.

That Wilkes was wrong in revealing as much of his own work to Ross as he did goes now without saying. He was indiscreet. Ross was exploring for a rival government and the United States had every right to expect the commander of its expedition to keep his own counsel. But Wilkes' letter reflected the fact that all men who go into Antarctic waters are essentially allies against that hostile environment. All help and aid are given freely for the problem of survival is uppermost in everyone's mind. As for revealing what land he had sighted, Wilkes realized his mistake when he reached the Sandwich Islands after leaving Sydney.

Ross had sailed along some of Wilkes' track and, using the positions Wilkes had given him, shown conclusively that no land existed in those precise spots. Ross had sailed into what is now named the Ross Sea, going eastward from longitude 160°East which is where Wilkes had sailed westward. Ross penetrated the great indentation—

the largest and deepest on that side of the continent—and made important landfalls that became the later claim of England to priority in the area. When Ross returned, he made it known that he had proved Wilkes false in a number of places.

The news got around rapidly. By the time Wilkes reached the Sandwich Islands, a fellow naval officer had spread the word that Ross had made a fool of Wilkes. Today it seems incredible that an officer of the United States Navy would injure both a colleague, the service and his country by accepting the claims of a foreign expedition commander before even talking with the United States commander. But the deed and the damage were done.

For years, Wilkes worked on the immense quantity of material he and his men had gathered. He wrote five volumes of narrative alone and the scientific reports, charts and oceanographic and navigational data kept coming in further volumes. Yet it was all to no avail. By some trick of the combination of circumstances, Wilkes sank further into oblivion as an explorer.

When the Civil War came, Wilkes was still a very active and irascible Navy officer. He served throughout that conflict, got himself in trouble again with the Navy Department and suffered another court-martial. When the Civil War ended, Wilkes went back to his monumental editing job of the volumes of the already forgotten expedition. Finally Congress refused to furnish more funds to publish additional volumes and the work came to a halt, though it was not complete by Wilkes' standards. In

1879, Rear Admiral Charles Wilkes, U.S.N. (ret.) died.

Yet the business of obliterating the results of his expedition continued with even greater vigor. Clements Markham, a powerful English explorer-patriot and geographer led the fight of a group of English geographers literally to erase Wilkes' discoveries from the maps and the records. He tried, unsuccessfully, to have the gold medal of the English Royal Geographic Society, which had been awarded to Wilkes, withdrawn. He urged English explorers in the Antarctic to check and refute as many of Wilkes' landfalls as possible. So as the nineteenth century drew to a close, the name of Wilkes and the credibility of his records was growing fainter and fainter. Markham as a contributor to an early edition of the *Encyclopaedia Britannica* ignored all of Wilkes' work in the Antarctic. His disciples followed his lead and as late as the first decade of the twentieth century, English—and world—geographic opinion held that Wilkes was at very best an inaccurate navigator, explorer and cartographer.

But the tide against Wilkes gradually turned. As some of his critics put down landfalls that later proved to be inaccurate, the entire question of positioning distant land by sighting across miles of Antarctic ice came under study. Two circumstances of the atmosphere in Antarctic regions produced the inaccuracies.

The first cause is the undreamed of clarity of the air in Antarctic regions. So free from dust and moisture is it at certain times over the ice shelves that objects judged by eye to be twenty or so miles away actually may lie more than a hundred miles distant. Thus, reliance on visual observation from a single position can cause tremendous errors.

The other phenomenon is a type of mirage known in high latitudes as "looming." As light is refracted or bent through layers of cold and warm air, a mirage sometimes occurs that makes distant objects appear to be raised above the horizon. In fact such mirages in the Antarctic are frequently so pronounced that mountains that are actually below the horizon of an observer may "loom" up or "mirage up" and appear to be only a few miles away.

Ross himself, as it turned out, had been deceived and had recorded land where it could not later be found. There are on record numerous examples of the visual trick the Antarctic plays on explorers and, on many occasions, men sledging across the ice have looked ahead and seen camp waiting for them at an apparent distance of only a few miles, but have had to travel another day or two to reach it. On some occasions it has caused the death of men —on others it has saved their lives. On one of Sir Ernest Shackleton's expeditions to the interior of the continent, he and his men were running out of food and could not find their next supply cache. Then, miraculously, in looking for it, they saw it miraged up but still beyond the horizon. But by taking a bearing on the mirage, they knew the direction to travel and eventually reached it and the food waiting for them. Without that mirage effect, they would have starved.

So while Wilkes' bearings or angles were correct, his estimation of distance to the sighted land was seriously wrong—as much as 200 miles wrong in some extreme cases. Where he placed land at 20 miles from a given ship's position Ross managed later to sail and disprove him. The land actually was present, but miles farther south than it appeared.

Had two of the squadron's ships sighted on the same mountain peak from a known distance apart they could have produced a triangle which would have shown the true distance of the peak from the vessels. But sailing separately, the ships had to rely on a single line of position where the angle or bearing could be relied upon but distance could not.

Fortunately for history, the intense competition among geographical explorers has subsided as most of the land masses of the planet have been allotted to one or another claimant. Emphasis today in the Antarctic is on scientific measurement and study of many things. Mapping still proceeds (and newcomers to the Antarctic are fooled as easily as Wilkes had been concerning the distance of objects sighted) but as the continent becomes more thoroughly known, Wilkes' work is finally being recognized. For he was the first explorer to understand that a vast southern continent exists.

Wilkes sailed into oblivion in 1838 because he competed with the English and French explorers, who felt they had a prior right to the area known as Antarctica because earlier explorers of those countries had first penetrated the region.

But if Wilkes had never gone near the Antarctic, his work in the Pacific and in the Oregon Territory would have assured him fame if he could have kept his peace with the Navy Department and his fellow officers. But being the kind of man he was, he did not avoid conflict nor did he see why another's opinion should stand in place of his own. So perhaps his oblivion of nearly a century was inevitable. But the stern, irascible figure of Wilkes refused to remain in limbo. He has gradually returned, his credibility restored to history, his records and honor intact, as the commander of a squadron of ships that sailed for four years to the ends of the earth and back on a great forgotten voyage.

ABOUT THE AUTHOR

William Bixby was born in San Diego, California, of a Navy family and grew up in California, Florida, and Tennessee where he attended public schools. He took an engineering degree in college and upon graduation in 1942 entered the service. He served first as a Signal Corps Officer and later transferred to the Air Corps. He served overseas as a pilot with the 8th Air Force in England. In 1945 he took up a career of journalism and worked for eight years as a magazine writer and associate editor on a number of New York publications.

In 1953 he decided to leave the city to teach and work on his own books. He settled in New England, where his family originated, and has taught variously in public and private schools in Vermont, Massachusetts, and Rhode Island. Presently he is a part-time instructor of physics at New Haven College, New Haven, Connecticut. Mr. Bixby is married and has two children: a son, William, Jr., and a daughter, Barbara.

INDEX

N

O

P

R

S

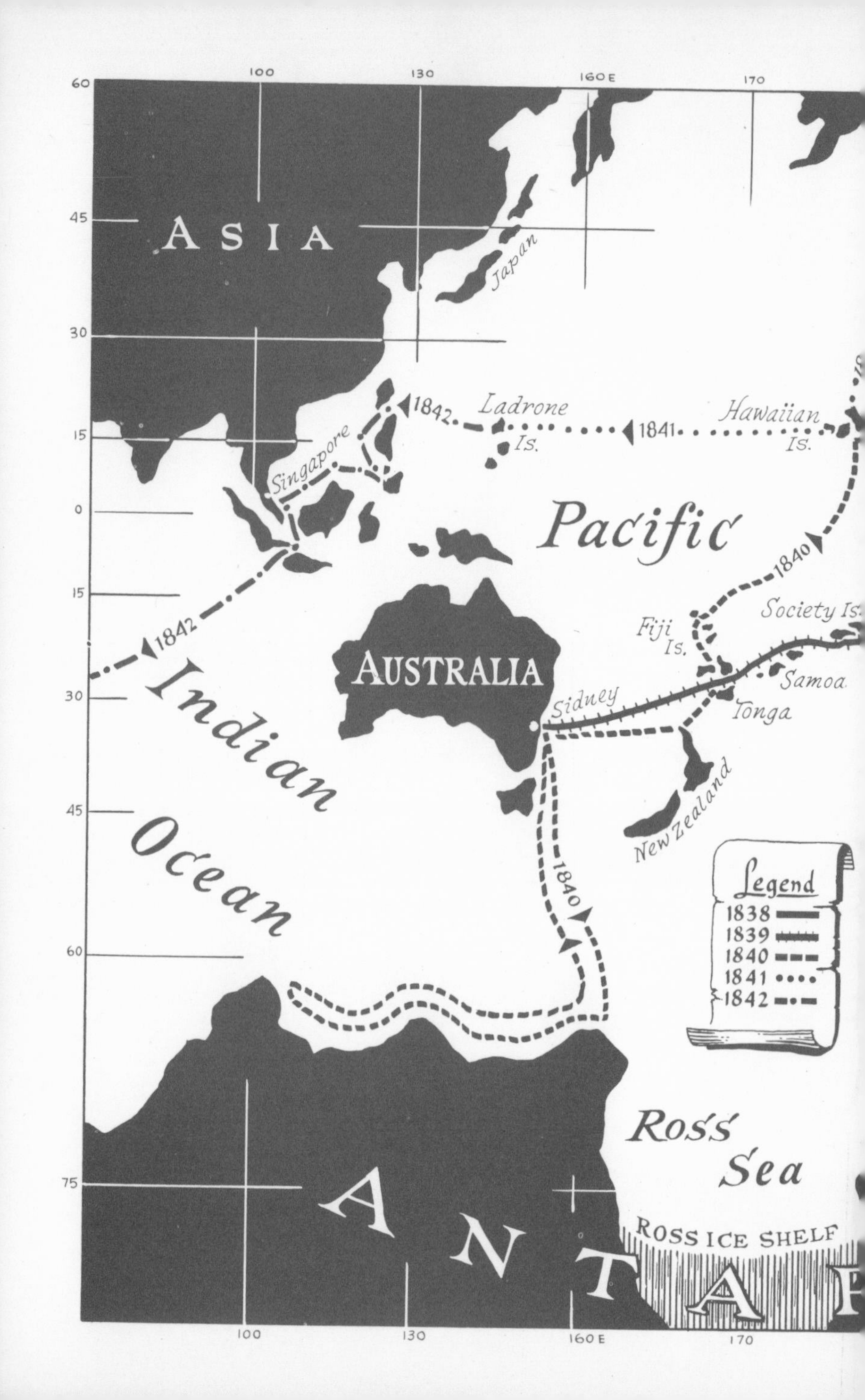

ASIA
Japan
Ladrone Is.
Hawaiian Is.
Singapore
Pacific
Fiji Is.
Society Is.
Samoa
Tonga
AUSTRALIA
Sidney
New Zealand
Indian Ocean
Ross Sea
ROSS ICE SHELF
ANTA
1842
1841
1840
Legend
1838
1839
1840
1841
1842
100
130
160 E
170
60
45
30
15
0
15
30
45
60
75

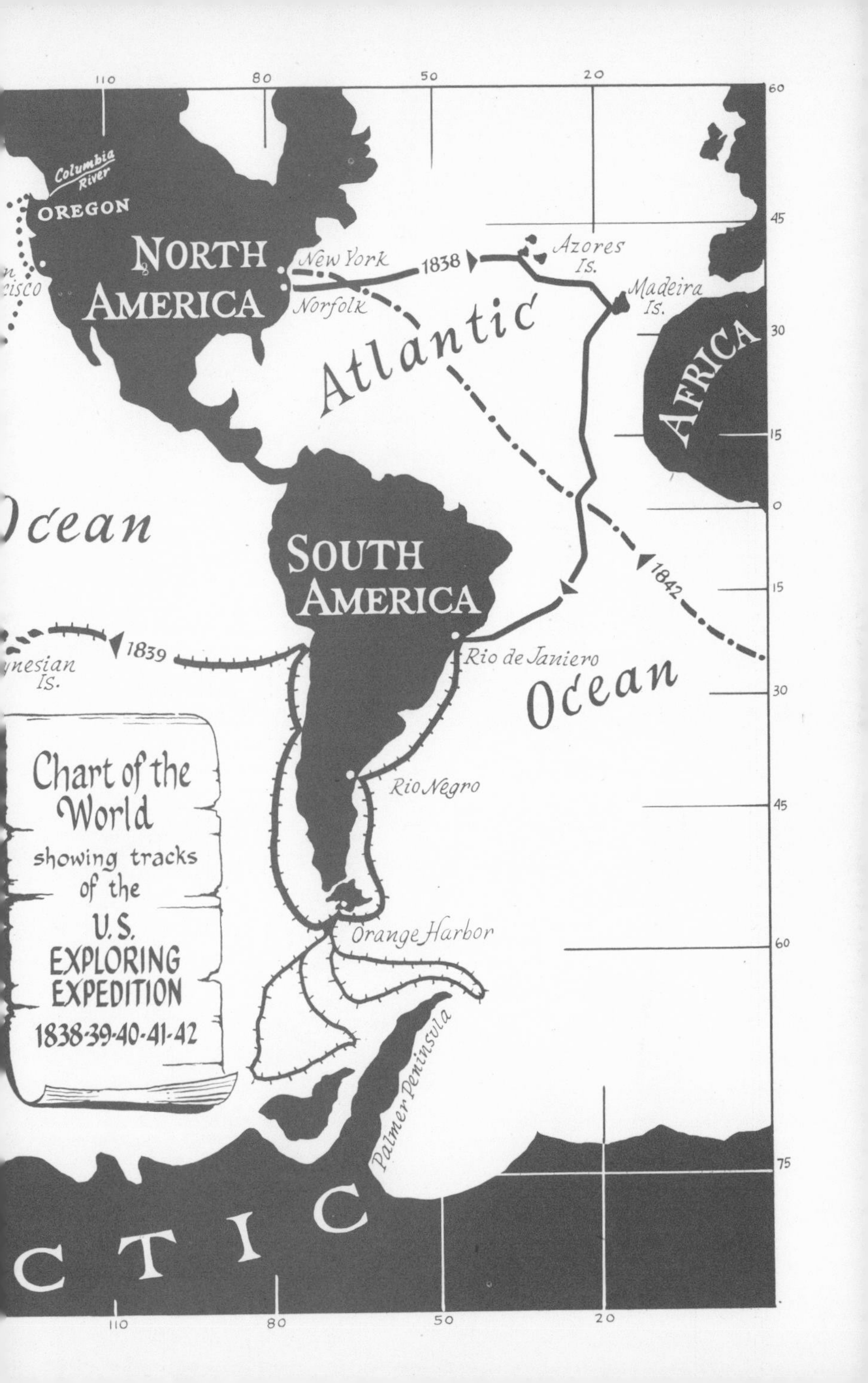

110
80
50
20
60
45
30
15
0
15
30
45
60
75
Columbia River
OREGON
NORTH AMERICA
New York
Norfolk
1838
Azores Is.
Madeira Is.
Atlantic
AFRICA
Ocean
SOUTH AMERICA
1842
1839
Is.
Rio de Janiero
Ocean
Rio Negro
Chart of the World showing tracks of the U.S. EXPLORING EXPEDITION 1838-39-40-41-42
Orange Harbor
Palmer Peninsula
C T I C
110
80
50
20